AS LUCK WOULD HAV

VANWELL
VOICES
of WAR

VERITY SWEENY PURDY

AS LUCK WOULD HAVE IT

ADVENTURES WITH THE
CANADIAN ARMY SHOW 1943-1946

Vanwell Publishing Limited

St. Catharines, Ontario

Vanwell Publishing acknowledges the financial support of the Government of Canada
through the Book Publishing Industry Development Program for our publishing activities.

Vanwell Publishing acknowledges the Government of Ontario through the Ontario Media
Development Corporation's Book Initiative.

Design: Linda Moroz-Irvine
Cover: All three photographs, Verity Sweeny.

Vanwell Publishing Limited
1 Northrup Crescent
P.O. Box 2131
St. Catharines, Ontario L2R 7S2
sales@vanwell.com
1-800-661-6136

In the United States:
P.O. Box 1207
Lewiston, NY 14092
USA

Printed in Canada

National Library of Canada Cataloguing in Publication

Purdy, Verity Sweeny, 1922-
        As luck would have it : adventures in the Canadian Army Show, 1938-1946 /
Verity Sweeny Purdy.

(Vanwell voices of war, ISSN 1498-8844)
ISBN 1-55125-051-9

        1. Purdy, Verity Sweeny, 1922- 2. Canadian Army Show--History.
3. Soldiers--Recreation--Canada--History--20th century. 4. World War, 1939-1945--
Theater and the war. I. Title. II. Series.

D810.E8P87 2003   940.53'088'7927   C2003-901464-9

CONTENTS

I recall with infinite appreciation the members of a
dedicated company of soldiers (especially Sully)
who made it their duty to lift the spirits of their
Comrades At Arms during WWII,
and I thank my brilliant and long-suffering
editor/agent Betty C. Keller, without whose support
I could never have written a book.

PROLOGUE

Tonight, having played to packed houses from coast to coast, The Canadian Army Show (CAS) is presenting its final performance at the Strand Theatre in Vancouver. The crowd is on its feet, clapping, shouting and whistling, drowning out composer Robert Farnon's full concert orchestra and the last, last, chorus of "Let's Make a Job of It Now." Shiny blue velours swoop in from either side of the proscenium arch, open again, and after several more noisy curtain calls, close on the show for the last time.

As Captain Robert Farnon once again lifts his baton, the theatre becomes hushed. Everyone stands at attention to sing robustly from the beginning to the end of Bob's full-bodied arrangement of "God Save the King." But they haven't finished cheering and, ignoring protocol, the audience starts calling and clapping again.

It has been a spectacular show from beginning to end and I have seen it all from the front row of the dress circle. Beside me stands the commanding officer of Canadian Army Shows, Major W. Victor George.

As the cheering continues, he guides me toward the exit. "What did you think of it?"

I have only just been introduced to this man by my Uncle Dick Bell-Irving, and here he is asking my opinion of the show! Of course, Major George knows that even though I am only twenty-one, I am a trained dancer and choreographer. Trying to sound professional, I manage some obvious remarks, but the show has been so good and I am on such a high that I can barely speak.

"It's so... big! So... polished!" I grab at words excitedly. "And...and screamingly funny. I mean..."

"I gather you liked it," says the major, grinning.

"Oh, yes!" I hear myself babbling the jargon of superlatives that I've grown used to in my three years of dancing in the U.S. "This show has class. The performers are all very talented." I can't stop my nervous chatter. "Thank you so much, Major George. It's a great production."

As we reach the foyer, the major stops abruptly and turns to face me. "Are you interested in joining the Army Show?" he asks. "Would you care to audition?"

I am momentarily without words. His questions are part of my own bigger question. But I collect my thoughts clearly enough to explain, "I expect to hear from The American Ballet Theatre at any moment about a contract with them."

"So I've heard."

"I'm sorry I can't answer you right this..."

"Well, let me know, will you? Ask your uncle to call me."

"Of course. Thank you for this evening. It was wonderful. I'll be in touch for sure."

The date of that performance was July 1943. As luck would have it, my life had reached a pivotal point when Major George asked me his questions. Behind me, I had five years of studying dance in England, another year at the BC Ballet School in Vancouver, a year in California dancing and studying with Bronislav Nijinskya and two years teaching and studying in Seattle. The question now before me was: what should I be doing for the rest of my life? Until that moment I had been seriously considering dancing with the American Ballet Theatre. But could my destiny lie with the Canadian Army Show?

CHAPTER 1

Family Album

I am Verity. Verity Sweeny. Oddly enough, I have no middle name. Born at home, on Barclay Street, Vancouver, B.C., in 1922, I came third in my family after my brothers Sedley Bell-Irving Sweeny and Malcolm Campbell Sweeny. Though we were an Irish clan, almost all the Sweenys had Campbell as an appendage.

Although he had several proper names, my father was known as Ben, his brother as Bimbo and their sister Dorothea Campbell as Doffie. My Sweeny grandfather, Campbell, born in Quebec, was married to Agnes Blanchard, an opera singer from Nova Scotia.

At about age seven, poor little Doffie developed a tubercular spine which twisted her body and restricted her growth. In those days one did not speak of such an illness, so my grandmother, dominant and socially correct, dreamed up the story that on one of their trips to England, Doffie had fallen off the Brighton Pier and injured her back on the stone steps. Once Bimbo and Ben, aged eleven and nine, had been shipped off to school in England, Agnes was free to travel with Doffie in search of a cure. Between sessions at hospitals, stretched and weighted or locked in a body cast (none of which solved the problem) her mother introduced Dorothea to voice teachers in France and Italy all of whom agreed that the youngster's contralto voice was exceptionally powerful and emotional. In every case, however, these maestros gave up on her training when it became obvious she couldn't breathe deeply enough to sustain quality on a long aria. Nevertheless, Doffie found friends and made her niche among artists and theatre people in many countries.

Tall, handsome and elegant, but a very gentle man, my grandfather Sweeny had brought the Bank of Montreal west (reaching British Columbia in 1887) and had later been appointed Bank of Montreal superintendent for the whole of British Columbia and the Yukon Territories. I didn't know my grandmother who was said to have died rather dramatically after playing and singing her own swan song sometime before I was born, but I remember Grandfather. After his death in 1928, Uncle Bimbo and my dad forfeited their shares of his estate in order to ensure a comfortable life for Doffie.

My mother was the eldest of four daughters, and sister to six brothers. Henry Ogle Bell-Irving, a Scot born in Dumfriesshire, had come to British Columbia around 1880 and, with money from his Scottish cousins, pioneered with great success in the development of the fishing industry. During the next two decades his wife, Marie Isabel del Carmen, delivered ten living children: Henry, Richard, Isabel, Roderick, Malcolm, Anita, Duncan, Mary, Aeneas, and Beatrice. Being the eldest girl, at an early age Isabel took on much of the responsibility of child-rearing. The Sweeny and Bell-Irving families belonged to the small group of Vancouver's socially elite. My mother and father knew each other from childhood.

In 1914, all of my uncles left Canada to fight for Britain on land, on sea and in the air. Dad was already over there, having gained a commission in the Royal Engineers upon his graduation from Royal

Military College, Kingston. Mum joined the V.A.D.s and followed the six Bell-Irving men (and her betrothed, Gerry Heath) to England. There she nursed wounded servicemen, several of whom were her brothers. One of Canada's early casualties was Gerry Heath. Uncle Duncan and Uncle Malcolm, both members of the Royal Flying Corps were seriously wounded. Malcolm lost a leg but survived a bullet in the head. Ben Sweeny was wounded in France. While on sick leave in London in 1916, he proposed to Isabel, his first love. They were married in 1917. My brother Sedley was born in England. Uncle Roderick lost his life close to the end of the war.

By the time I was born, the Great Depression was taking what joy was left in life from all but the very rich. My father, schooled in England and trained as a military engineer, had positively no business sense. Try as he always did, he found it exasperatingly difficult to make enough money to feed his family, let alone *make* money the way the Bell-Irvings seemed able to do. Soon after my sister, named Dorothea Moira after Doffie, arrived in 1925, Dad finally settled for a well-paid position as chief engineer for a mining company in Anyox, of all the God-forsaken places, near the Alaskan border. There were whispers suggesting trouble between my parents, but I have read letters Dad wrote to Mum and some to us children that she kept, and I know, deep down, the whispers were wrong. However, much as we adored our Dad we saw mighty little of him in those days.

On the other hand, Grandfather Bell-Irving provided luxuries in the form of a summer paradise called Pasley Island that he'd bought in 1910 and on which he built a cottage for each of his children as they married and had families. I remember counting twenty-five first cousins who spent summers at Pasley, an island of about three hundred pristine acres in the mouth of Howe Sound barely twenty miles from Vancouver Harbour. Grandfather also provided a boat with skipper to ferry us to and fro with all our supplies. He was usually aboard when the *Emoh* (*home* spelled backwards) arrived in North Bay on Saturday afternoons from June until August. Of course, Mum had accepted a cottage and spent summers there, partly because she felt responsible for looking after Grandfather since Granny, being ill—or was she just too tired?—no longer visited the island.

Chung and his son Lui took care of Pasley year round. They also tended extensive vegetable gardens and fruit trees. *Cum Spring*, one of Grandfather's cannery boats brought sheep, chickens and Jersey cows for everyone to enjoy; and sometimes a pony or two. I spent the first eleven joyous summers of my life at Pasley totally unaware that most other children were not so bountifully blessed. It must have been hard for Mum because Dad could seldom join us; and when he did, Grandfather usually put him to work with other weekending fathers, felling trees or painting dinghies, opening trails or digging a new well, when all Dad wanted was to visit with his family. Poor Dad. He never complained. How could he? Long ago he had refused a position with H. Bell-Irving and Company.

As the depression deepened, businesses closed. Dad was without a job again and had to sell the Green Winter House as we called our house on Barclay Street. We had been living, almost rent free, in Grandfather Bell-Irving's guest house on Harwood Street when the head of the Bell-Irving clan died. Soon after that, Dad moved us out of Vancouver into a twelve-dollars-a-month log cabin on a chicken farm at Gibson's Landing, a village on the mainland a few miles north of Pasley. That there was no running water or that we had to use coal-oil lamps was fine for us children, but must have been hard on Mum, who had recently given us a new baby brother, Roger Douglas Campbell Sweeny. At Gibson's Landing, Sedley, Malcolm, Moira and I climbed up a long, steep hill to the schoolhouse wearing hand-me-down uniforms from the private schools of our Bell-Irving cousins. No wonder the local kids giggled.

Dad, who stayed in Vancouver doing carpentry and other odd jobs well beneath his dignity, couldn't often afford the ferry fare to visit us. We missed him terribly. I guess he finally asked his sister Doffie, in Australia at the time and spending the Sweeny estate quite recklessly, to help with the education of her nephews. Totally unexpectedly, Doffie chose to become my guardian and to pay for putting me through ballet school, not in Australia but in London where England's first ballerina, Phyllis Bedells, taught the Royal Academy method of classical dance. No one asked how I felt about it, but the next spring I was told that in September I would leave home to live with Doffie and study to become a dancer.

I have to admit that the idea of learning more about dancing had great appeal. I had always flitted about as children do. Encouraged by Grandfather Bell-Irving, I often danced for him and his friends to beautiful music he played on the wind-up gramophone. I believe he paid for my dancing lessons from Miss Pumphrey and he himself taught me to skate on frozen Lost Lagoon. No wonder I adored him. With neither Mum nor Dad to see me onto the train—Dad couldn't take the time from his new teaching job at St. George's School for Boys, and Mum couldn't face sending me away—I set off on the first long journey of my life.

For the next two years, I lived at Cheyne Cottage with Doffie, meeting many of her Chelsea friends, tutored in the forenoon by her sundry acquaintances and studying dance from one until five, and spending wonderful holidays with relatives, mostly Bell-Irvings, in Scotland.

During that time Malcolm, known as Mickie, unconscionably beautiful with a personality to match, chose at sixteen to become a sea captain and, with Dad's blessing if not Mum's, to work his way to Britain on a tramp steamer out of Vancouver. Mickie and I had good times in London while Doffie saw to it he got properly outfitted to join HMS *Worcester*, a mercantile training ship at Greenhythe on the River Thames. On several occasions, Doffie took me by bus to teas aboard the *Worcester*. Once, my girlfriend Mary Stirling and I skipped class to visit these glamourous cadets Mickie introduced us to; one of them was Hamid Kedjar, the ex-Crown Prince of Persia. We weren't smart and were found out. For a time I was forbidden to see Mary. Another time, Mickie came with me to Scotland. He was not as enthralled as I by the opulence and grandeur of some of our Scottish cousins.

The following summer Malcolm was invited, along with fourteen other teenaged boys, to crew on the racing schooner *Altair*. She belonged to an engineer friend of Dad's and was scheduled to sail (without auxiliary power or two-way radio) to the Azores and back to Britain, a voyage that should have taken about six weeks. Five weeks into the journey we had a letter that Malcolm had mailed when they made port in the Azores. Any time now they should arrive in Portsmouth. But they didn't come back. They just didn't come back. Week after week and month after month, we talked about the possible reasons for their delay and kept hoping. No one ever mentioned to me the possibility, the probability or the inescapable reality. People just stopped asking, "What news of your brother?" I grew quieter and wearier and began to have colds. I lost weight and had to struggle to get through my classes. I know now how much effort went into searching for *Altair*, but no one put me into the picture during the search or later.

The next summer I went home to Vancouver to have my tonsils removed and felt the terrible pain and sadness of Dad and Mum and Moira. Mum's hair had turned white. Someone had sent Sedley the money for his fare home from Royal Military College, Kingston, where, in Dad's footsteps, he was studying to become an engineer. Roger was too young to understand what had happened but he seemed to know not to pester Mum. Still, I never heard a word about Malcolm's death. There was no service. In September, Sedley went back to college and I returned to classes, exams and competitions. Slowly, reality set in. I began to work at a deeper level of feeling.

In 1938, when the Second World War seemed inevitable, my parents insisted I come home. Once again, I had to leave behind the world to which I then belonged. Who would be there for me at home? Moira. That I knew for sure. What I didn't know until I got home was that Moi, who'd been following my studies, had theoretically raced ahead of me in many ways. She'd become a full-blown balletomane. She knew much more about dance companies and their stars than I did. She could read a symphony score, and belonged to the Sir Ernest McMillan Club. Though not a serious dancer, she had been taking lessons. We practised together in the big studio bedroom we shared in our parents' North Vancouver house. She and I discussed vague ideas about my career, for which Mum and Dad apparently had no vision. Conscious that I was losing something precious, I tried several local dance schools, but none of them offered what I needed. I seemed to exist in limbo, but sometimes momentous movements in our lives can be initiated by the simplest things...perhaps a phone call from a relative.

My aunt, Bea Abercrombie, was responsible for putting me on the path to June Roper.

CHAPTER 2

"Get That Leg Up, Honey:" The B.C. School of Dancing

"Verity, this is Bea Abercrombie." My mother's sister spoke sharply into the phone. "I'm not happy to hear by my grapevine that you are looking in the wrong places for a dance teacher. You've been home from England for months. Why haven't you been to see June Roper?"

The woman my aunt referred to was an American dance teacher who, in 1935, had been hired by the Vancouver Junior League to direct their annual fund-raiser. She had rented a studio and auditioned local students to perform in the production, which was so successful that, three months later when she opened her own B.C. School of Dancing, many of those students had flocked to her door. I had been training in England at that time and had heard rumours that her behaviour was underhanded. Now, four years later, here was my Aunt Bea suggesting I should take lessons from this notorious woman. I explained my objections.

"Rubbish! The other teachers are just jealous because she's doing so well. Don't listen to that stuff. After all your wonderful training in England it's a crime to be letting that work go. Get smart, my dear. Don't waste any more time."

I had been home from England since July 1938 and it was now mid-September. I was getting soft from all this time without real direction, but didn't know what to do about it. I was waiting for someone to tell me, I suppose. They always had in the past.

"You should be dancing every day," Aunt Bea said.

"Wouldn't I love that!" I replied. "At home, Moira's the only one who mentions my career."

"My poor girl, your parents haven't a clue how important your career is, or how to guide you. You'll have to get a part-time job and start taking lessons right away. Come and see me at Carmichael's. We'll have a chat."

My elegant and socially prominent Aunt Bea, recently separated from her husband John Abercrombie, lived in a charming boarding house on Haro street in Vancouver's West End. A big old place, respectable but somewhat run-down, it was owned by a Mrs. Carroll who loved to cook and whose clientele consisted of two young businessmen, my aunt, and two widows with "uppity" backgrounds who had fallen on hard times, along with their out-of-university but as yet unmarried offspring. These were Mrs. Hulbert and her twenty-three-year-old twins Ethel and Anna, and Mrs. Jollivet plus her son Lawrence who was known as Jolly and was about the age of the twins.

Bea managed Carmichael's, a posh silversmith shop on Howe Street. When I met her there the next day she offered me a part-time job cleaning silver and said she could pay me just enough for one ballet lesson a day. Then, even though I was still not convinced that June Roper had behaved fairly, Bea hurried me off to meet the woman.

At first I was critical of June's American accent, her sleek, aqua silk "pyjamas," white angora pullover, exotic makeup and scarlet fingernails. My prejudices made it difficult for me to see the real person, but if I had held a picture of an ogre in my subconscious or feared she would be overpowering, that was quickly dispelled. "Sit down, honey," she said as she led me into her office. I wondered if Bea might have phoned her. Within minutes we were excitedly sharing opinions on dance and discipline. I realized she knew and loved her business.

"The kids work on their own from the time the studio opens at seven-thirty," she explained. "If ya wanna get in shape, ya bedder be there. Class starts at ten."

Within a week, Bea had convinced my parents that I must attend the B.C. School of Dancing and that they should finance a room for me at the boarding house. Happy as I had been to come home from England three months earlier, I left again without regret, glad to have my career back on track.

One week of working with June Roper was all I needed to recognize an extraordinarily talented person and a demanding teacher. About five-foot-five or-six, June was taller than average for a ballet dancer in those days. She wasn't exactly plump, but she was voluptuous, long legged and as limber as an acrobat. In her mid-thirties she could—and often did—demonstrate what she meant by "Get that leg up real high, honey." June wasn't pretty but she was glamourous, and she dressed to match her natural auburn colouring and extravagant personality. In applying her elaborate makeup, she paid special attention to her blue-green eyes, and the cheeks of her round face were almost as pink as her full lips, but the makeup never quite obliterated her friendly freckles. June's was a Hollywood smile that showed all her snowy teeth. Sometimes after class she would stand re-arranging her long and naturally curly hair before the studio mirror. Combing out a thick strand, she'd roll it up again over two fingers and pin the fat sausage-curl behind a rather protruding ear. About her face she arranged shorter ringlets and kiss curls which managed to stay immaculately in place even though she occasionally got carried away during a lesson demonstrating to us how she wanted something done.

As a youngster, June had been a pupil of the English ballet-master Ernest Belcher at his Los Angeles school. Unfortunately, lack of family finances had forced her early into the professional world where she and her several partners, including her brother Ken, enjoyed successful careers performing all over the United States and in Europe as highly sophisticated night-club adagio teams or a trio. Adagio was new at the time—a sensual dance-form combining pointe-work, acrobatics, aerobatics (flying through the air from one partner to another), high lifts and spins. June's costumes were voluminous and often transparent and, judging from pictures, she knew how to use her eyes. But even in those days, she must have had other dreams because in Vancouver, as traditionally as she remembered, she was teaching classical Russian ballet.

Despite my attempts to work at home, I was badly out of practice by the time I started with June, but once she knew my background, she put me into her professional class—an hour and a half each morning. At first, having lived in a cocoon of British influence, I was particularly aware of June's American way of speech. My own name, from her lips sounded like "Verdi." But although she so completely Americanized the French ballet terms that they were barely recognizable, we invariably understood each other and laughed at our differences.

Though its inconspicuous entrance was tucked between the back exit of the Orpheum Theatre and a greasy spoon restaurant on Seymour street at Robson, inside, June's Ballet School was surprisingly spacious. Beyond a meagre waiting room, a door on the left led past Hope Beasley's small costume and sewing-room into the business office. From there, the teachers and Mrs. Scott, the accompanist, entered the front of the main studio next to the piano. This large room, big enough to handle thirty or so students, had a ten-foot ceiling, and the right kind of wooden floor for dance practice. The front wall was fully mirrored and there were lightweight but strong barres of two heights—the top barre higher, I noted, than was customary in England. There was a second, marginally smaller, practice room beyond the main studio, and beyond it, dressing rooms—invariably crowded—and the loo.

A modest hand-basin hung against the dressing room wall but there were no showers. With sweat saturating our practice clothes and the towels that hung on hooks everywhere and drying on our bodies time after time, a stink inevitably permeated the back premises, made worse by the fact that there were few windows at this end of the building. The air had little chance to circulate.

Yet there was something even more odoriferous than stale sweat that hit the nostrils upon entering the second studio: the powerful, acid-sweet reek of grapefruit. This was part of a weight-control formula practised by all the serious students, which allowed nothing but that fruit before 2:00 p.m. While European and English dancers were still content to look Degas-ish, rounded and fully female, George Ballanchine in the United States had already begun to set a new body style, that of the wraith. It had caught on in New York, was spreading fast in North America and would ultimately change most sylph-like dancers to skeletons world-wide, leading to epidemics of anorexia and other health disorders in the dance world.

June herself remained pleasantly curvaceous, but her emphasis on producing a streamlined body was far stronger than I had previously experienced. As I was embarrassingly softer and plumper than my new fellow-dancers, I quickly took to their routine, happily adding to the stink by another five or six grapefruit per day.

Although my job cleaning silver and doing other chores at Carmichael's paid just enough for my daily professional class, quite soon opportunities arose for me to pay for extra lessons by demonstrating at afternoon classes. I also began coaching younger students, something I had been commended for doing well during my last year in England. This work not only equalled the value of the professional class but gave me the hours of physical work I needed. Finally, this meant giving up my job at Carmichael's but Bea, having given me the shove I needed, was happy to release me.

Much of what June taught was excitingly new to me. My classical training had been predominantly Royal Academy, a rather stately and reserved style, but I had also studied the Italian and Russian methods. Although I thought June's style lacked classical finesse and she neglected to correct body line, her work was flashy, technically brilliant and full of enthusiasm.

I recognized that in June's commercially flavoured approach there was much of value that I must learn, and once I began to really know her professional students, a valuable exchange of ideas took place amongst us. It was particularly surprising and flattering when one morning June paused in the barre-work and suggested everyone take a look at the way I was doing my grandes battements derrière.

"See how Verdi keeps her hip down. She kicks real straight back. Some a you kinda let yer leg swing out sideways." Another time she spoke of the smooth movement of my arms and noted that I held them slightly lower than my shoulders. Heady praise for a sixteen-year-old.

But until I learned some of their tricks, I was in awe of June's students. They spun like skaters and could balance on one pointe almost indefinitely. One of the things that assisted them to accomplish these neat effects was the make of pointe-shoes they wore. "Barney's blocks," which came from an American cobbler, were expensive but long-lasting and much heavier than any I had ever worn. They had wide tips covered with suede and such pronounced built-in arches that, once up, it was difficult to come off pointe. And they fit longer than one's own foot, which left room for a considerable cushion of lamb's-wool. As the shoe aged and softened, one could press the pointe hard to the ground and by swizzling it around, create a sizable platform on which to spin three or four times without difficulty! I tried Barney's once, and though I could see some advantages, I found them heavy and cumbersome, particularly on the flat.

In contrast, I wore a lightly blocked Italian slipper made by Porcelli in London. Exactly the length of the wearer's foot, the shoe could be quickly "broken in" and made quiet. With only a breath of lamb's-wool between the toes and the block, this softer, more flexible shoe forced the wearer to rely almost entirely on muscular strength to work en pointe. Rather than depending on my shoes, I strove to pull my whole body up off them. It's true my shoes wore out comparatively fast. Though cheap, they were made on my own last, half a dozen pairs at a time and sent from England by mail. Fortunately, during my year with June Roper I discovered lightweight American Capezio shoes and an imported British brand called Frederick Freed. Because flat-work is more difficult in blocked shoes with their stiff, narrow soles than in soft leather shoes, for the sake of good balance June made us wear our old pointe shoes for flat-work until they literally fell apart.

June taught the usual plié, ronde de jambe, battement and frappé exercises but not nearly so many slow and careful foot, body and arm placements as I was accustomed to. Every exercise seemed to empha-size limberness and the development of muscles to attain high exten-sions. We did miles of forward and back bends and endless stretching of legs along the high barres. In centre floor the combinations consist-ed of bourées, jetés, pirouettes, long-held poses en pointe in arabesque, and tour-jetés which had particular arm movements with rather frilly hand positions but the whole effect was lively and fast-moving. The dancers certainly could spin and leap and balance like no others I had seen. And what's more, they could stop, as June put it, "on a dime." She taught a tough class but her criticism wasn't unkind. Within an atmosphere totally free from jealousy, she fed her eager stu-dents dazzling technique and showmanship, and, in retrospect, I real-ize I entered the B.C. School of Dancing at its absolute peak.

Once I was used to the earliness of the morning workout I wouldn't have missed it for anything. At least ten of the senior stu-dents took advantage of the free second studio every day, each one working on his or her own technique. After an hour or more of near silence at the barre we began to work together centre floor sharing our difficulties and small successes. The boys taught me lifts and throws they'd learned from June's instructor of adagio, Jerry Mathisen, and astonished me with their own spins—four, five and six done with the supporting heel barely off the floor, a masculine trick that was new to me. The girls showed me how balance on one pointe was achieved by finding centre on both feet and then very slowly moving the weight onto only one pointe and even more slowly, with the back arched and the arms held very still, lifting the other leg into arabesque, meanwhile adjusting the body weight slightly forward. Speed was their key to good pirouettes. Attack and the tightness of the arm position—middle finger-tips on thighs or on the point of the shoulder—also insured bril-liance. But our balletic terms were quite different. In my English/French vocabulary fast spins using both pointes were called deboulle; June called them chenne. What I knew as enchainements, they all called combinations. To them bourrées were toe-runs. I soon switched over to their modern terms.

I was pleased when one after the other my new friends asked me to show them the method of arms I used and to explain how I "moved from one step to another with flow." We began to talk about the "why" of movement, the warm and cool parts of the body, the sensitivity of hands. I showed them many of the Greek body-lines derived from ancient friezes on the Parthenon that I had learned while studying the Revived Greek Dance syllabus in London. This dance form had helped me understand natural contra-body movement and continuous motion.

June polished the skills of the several capable male dancers studying with her in order to give her female dancers the lavish support she wanted for them. As well, she had approached the Provincial Recreation Department and enticed several young physical-education teachers-in-training to take up ballet dancing. With their brawn and her extensive knowledge of lifts, it was now possible for her senior students to perform exciting sequences such as the "Polovotsian Dances" from *Prince Igor*.

By enlisting the aid of her many friends, June created other professional venues for her dancers. Thanks to her warm relationship with Orpheum Theatre manager Ivan Ackeray, she supplied short, live shows that were presented there before movies à la Radio City, New York. Ivan also made the Orpheum available for the elegant "Stars of Tomorrow" school recitals for which June groomed her up-and-coming professionals.

Of the two brothers who ran the Commodore Ballroom, Nick Kogas was her chosen contact. Through him she arranged regular cabarets for the Commodore with generous casts and every type of dance entertainment—Hawaiian, Spanish and a jazzy March Militaire, which was tap on pointe.

All these performances were, of course, amateur—we didn't get paid. But we felt and danced like pros by arranging to have our publicity pictures taken by Artona. June said he was "the only theatrically aware photographer in town."

Vancouver was a thriving centre of the arts in those days. More professional performers played the theatres in one month then than appear today in a whole year. Hugh Pickett and Gordon Hilker, two of the impresarios who brought fine artists to the city and regularly presented big ballet companies, knew how to publicize them astutely so as to provide full houses. June Roper seldom missed a performance, and she had such a facile brain she could memorize whole chunks of the ballets, which she then taught to us in the studio.

Although I was once again fully focused on my dancing career, a small part of me was seriously considering marriage.

I had met Pat Ainley in the summer of 1938, very soon after my return from England. He had come to Pasley Island as the guest of my cousin Constance Bell-Irving and her fiancé Rodney Browne. I had first seen Pat in the firelight of my Uncle Dick's cottage where, on the evening of my arrival, I had been invited to a party. Sipping a hot rum toddy on my cushion on the floor, I was glancing around to see who I might recognize when I found myself looking into the dark and twinkling eyes of a young man I didn't know. It felt as though he had been waiting for me to notice him. He smiled slightly and though I dropped my eyes, he was still watching when I looked up.

We didn't actually speak that evening, but I learned next day from Con that Pat was twenty-two and a UBC grad. She added that he would be staying at their cottage until the end of August. Her grin seemed to say "See what you can do, kid!"

Summer was half over, the Pasley meadow was yellow and the American Beauty roses, garlanding as I remembered them from one high post to another along the vegetable garden fence, had faded. But crickets sang in the afternoon and everyone swimming from the float looked tanned. Friends or family, they all seemed glad that I had come home. It was there I met Pat. He was the handsomest thing I'd ever seen, and as we swam together toward North Point, I showed him my sleekest strokes and porpoise dives. Later, I laid my towel on the float to sunbathe beside him.

From then on, our paths crossed almost daily, for any number of unlikely reasons. I needed help to paint the lean-to bathroom at my mother's cottage; Pat just happened to drop by. Or I was out to catch the ponies. There he was again: would he ride with me to deliver a message to my cousins at South Bay? He seemed delighted to oblige. In this simple but exciting way, I enjoyed the remainder of a perfect summer.

In September, when the cottages were closed up for the winter and the islanders had returned to city living, Con gave a dinner party at her parents' house in the west end of Vancouver. She invited me and, because my parents' home in North Vancouver was so remote, said I should stay the night. Although I bought a cocktail dress—two shades of blue silk sheer—for the occasion, I've forgotten who provided the money for it. Certainly I had none of my own.

There among the guests I saw Pat. Several times our eyes met across the huge dining table, and after a leisurely dinner when everyone headed downtown to the Commodore Ballroom, it was he who drove me in his father's pale blue convertible to my first public dance. "Mart Kenney and his Western Gentlemen" filled the bandstand and their music was perfect for my mellowing mood. Once Pat and I faced each other on the dance floor we melted together in perfect rhythm. A solemnity that needed no words descended upon us.

An English graduate, Pat was decidedly literate. As our friendship grew, he introduced me to Maugham and Huxley whose work we discussed at length. We climbed Grouse Mountain, attended the ballet and discovered new trails in Stanley Park. I was mad about Pat, and he did nothing to discourage me.

Mrs. Carroll's boarding house was less than a block away from Pat's parents' house on Barclay Street, and soon after I began my studies at the B.C. School of Dancing I had a weekly invitation to dine with them. Dr. and Mrs. Ainley welcomed me warmly, and I believed my relationship with Pat was secure. Though the word had never been mentioned, I had begun to assume we were heading for marriage. That dream was soon shaken when one evening Pat casually mentioned that he would soon be leaving to complete his doctorate at Harvard. This announcement came as a surprise but, so far as I was concerned, it only meant waiting a few years—as long as Canada didn't get pulled into a war.

However, it did start me thinking. Under the circumstances, shouldn't Pat really be joining a regiment? All the other men I could think of had enlisted. Even veterans of the last war—Dad and his brother, Uncle Bims, and Mum's brothers Henry, Duncan and Aeneas—had all taken up their reserve ranks. My own brother Sedley was in his last year at Military College and all male cousins were heading into the services. Even the other girls I knew planned to join as soon as they were old enough. I knew that people who didn't take sides were called pacifists, and I'd heard the word used derogatively about Americans. However, critical as I was of Pat at that moment, I didn't make the obvious comparison with my own behaviour. All that season I, too, was focused on my career.

With the coming of summer in 1939, I returned to Pasley Island. I expected to see Pat whenever he visited my cousins, but, although he spent two weekends there, both times he avoided me. Because his strange behaviour was turning my life upside down—implying that I had said the wrong thing or done something to offend him—I tried in every way I could to pin him down to a reasonable conversation. But he was indifferent, sarcastic and impatient to get away from me.

At the end of his second visit I watched the water-taxi *Tymac* pull out from the Pasley float, taking away this hurtful man. I waved. Pat turned his back on me. His body seemed to have shrunk, his brightness had disappeared. Suddenly I despised him. Feeling like a fool, I left the "farewell crowd" on the wharf and went to Mum's house to hide my misery, shame and anger. In late July I heard from Con that Pat was on his way to university in the USA. I asked, but he had left no message for me.

That summer we also said goodbye to my brother Sedley. He had graduated in the spring from Royal Military College in Kingston, Ontario, and before heading to Halifax and shipping out to England to take up a commission with the Royal Engineers, he spent the last part of his pre-service leave at Pasley. In August we waved him farewell with heightened awareness of the likelihood of his early involvement in a war.

For the next few weeks I remained at the island with Mum, Moira, and my youngest brother, Roger. Early one morning, a very large seaplane taxied into the island's north bay. By the time it had docked, dwarfing the boats there, all of us had gathered on the float to greet the new arrivals. Out of the huge body clambered my mother's brother, Uncle Duncan, a First World War air ace, still lame from serious war wounds, but back in uniform.

The plane, a First World War Royal Canadian Air Force Grumman Goose, had brought Billy Bishop (the First World War Canadian hero who had downed more German planes than any other pilot) and his son, Art, from Ottawa to Vancouver the previous day. My uncle (aide de camp to the Governor General, the Earl of Athlone) and young Art Bishop were accompanying the RCAF crew on a sea-landing practice flight which naturally dropped in at Pasley Island where Uncle Duncan's two daughters Liz and Trish were staying. The girls had planned to catch a ride back to Vancouver on *Tymac*, but an offer of a lift in the Goose sounded like much more fun. Uncle told us that the craft would be returning the Bishops to Ottawa next day, and Art added that the flight could connect with another to Halifax where it would be possible to put a letter aboard a ship. Did anyone have mail they wanted sent to England in a hurry?

"Duncan," called my mother, "can the crew take a letter to Sedley? He's on his way to his regiment at Chatham right this moment!"

My uncle assured her that a letter could be delivered in England within ten days. Everyone added their bit to Mum's scribble written right there on the float and watched her write Air Mail in large letters on the envelope. Though I found this example of speed exciting right then, it brought England and the likelihood of war frighteningly closer.

August was a sad month. Dad, having remobilized, once again held the rank of major and was on Vancouver Island with a gunnery unit. It was not the posting he wanted, but his old company wouldn't take him then–perhaps because he was forty-seven–though he later made the transfer to command his original engineers unit. Most other Pasley men had departed the island. The remaining adults, preoccupied with world affairs, stayed indoors to listen to their battery radios.

One morning, with the sun's rays softened by smoke from distant forest fires, Mum and I swam out into deep water from the only float not stranded on the beach by the outgoing tide. Later we sat on our towels in the sun listening to the quiet language of ducks and seagulls preening on distant rocks.

The stillness was broken by a man's voice which grew louder, cutting the air with a crackling sound as Con's younger brother Ian came down from their family cottage carrying his radio. Crossing the meadow, he descended the steps which led to the floats. This sort of noise would not normally have been acceptable on the island, but even Mum was keen to hear the commentator's sombre voice. There, on the float, on September third, 1939, we three listened to the listless voice of Neville Chamberlain on the BBC. "We were in consultation all day yesterday with the French Government and we felt that the intensified action which the Germans were taking against Poland allowed no delay in making our position clear." Speaking in a melancholic voice, he went on to say, "...that unless the German Government...had suspended all aggressive action against Poland...His Majesty's Government would, without hesitation, fulfil their obligation to Poland."

"Does that mean Britain will send troops to defend Poland?" I asked Mum, but before she could answer, the prime minister continued,

"...that unless not later than 11:00 a.m., British Summer Time today, third September, satisfactory assurances...have reached His Majesty's Government in London, a state of war will exist between the two countries as from that hour. No such undertaking was reached by the time stipulated. Consequently, this country is at war with Germany.

"This is a sad day for all of us," he said, "and to none is it sadder than to me..."

That morning must have been tough for Con and Ian. Their brother Dick had enlisted in the Royal Canadian Navy and so had Con's husband of only a few months, Rodney Browne. For Mum and me, it was Dad and Sedley who were soon to join the battle. Though I might be excused my lack of understanding because none of the disturbing aspects of the First World War had ever been spoken about by my parents, I later realized how packed with déjà vu Mum's emotions must have been on that day.

Until that day I had assumed that this safe and idyllic Pasley life was my heritage. Now as the heaviness of the world situation pressed in on me, even Pasley seemed threatened. Listening to the ongoing broadcast, I understood that for all of us a point of no return had already been reached. For a moment I sensed the panic of the British who must at last face their worst fears.

But my thoughts quickly returned to the comparative safety of the island. Nothing would touch us here. Less interested in the war than in my own life, I was still searching my wounded pride for the real reason behind Pat's desertion. It wouldn't have surprised me to learn that Pat had found me just too young and ignorant—he was considerably older than I and had far more formal education—or it could have been something to do with his choosing not to serve his country. I tried to remember some critical remark I may have made. Perhaps he simply could not tolerate the patriotic furore of my family.

Whatever his reason, I believed I had been found unworthy. In the end, I turned to hard work as the best medicine for my pain. In September 1939, I returned to Mrs. Carroll's boarding house and the B.C. School of Dancing. Except for Sundays with Mum and Moira in North Vancouver, every day of the week was fully scheduled at the school. In the spring of 1940 I danced a piece of my own choreography in June's "Stars of Tomorrow." For this two-and-a-half-minute variation to a nocturne by Chopin, I wore a floating sea-green tu-tu I had made on Bea's dressmaker's dummy. June was always enormously encouraging and at the end of my solo when I flew past the place where she watched from the wings, I heard her shout: "Bravo, Verdi. You danced just like Baron Ova!"

It was typical of June that she could not pronounce Baronova correctly, but her generosity always astonished me. I wanted to cry. I wished I had asked my close family to come and see me dancing, but I was in some other world from them, or they from me. Following that performance, to my embarrassment but huge delight, I was met in the theatre dressing room by a comedic contingent from the boarding house. Costumed to represent a circus barker, a washerwoman and a clown, Jolly, Ethel and Anna, each with a spiel to fit their characters, made a big act of bowing and scraping as they presented me with bouquets of tired flowers festooned with toilet paper. Then, grabbing me, my costumes and my makeup box, they continued their noisy show up the stairs, out into the rain and all the way home down the middle of Haro Street. Together we laughed and sang and danced under umbrellas as the night sky splashed upon us.

The whole of June Roper's spectacular teaching career lasted barely ten years, but during that time she put Vancouver dancers into orbit like rockets, sending them wherever they genuinely fit. The first pupils to sign contracts with Colonel de Basil's Russian Ballet Company had been Pat Meyers and Rosemary Deveson, entirely different in style from each other but both exceptionally talented. In fact, I had seen both of them perform solos with that company at Covent Garden a week or so before I left England. During my stay at the B.C. School, Yvonne de Carlo went to the Florentine Gardens Theatre Restaurant and thence to the movies, several adagio dance teams went "on the road," and one dancer joined Sally Rand's troupe. June arranged auditions with major dance companies for Audree Thomas, Joy Darwin and Jean Hunt, Duncan McGillvray, Robert Lindgren and Ian Gibson among many others from the professional class, all of whom hit the big time out of little Vancouver. And that spring, when she thought I was ready, June encouraged me to go to Hollywood to study with Bronislav Nijinskaya.

I didn't know then that June's own career had been hampered by her mother's and her own ill health. I did know that some days she suffered quite badly with rheumatic pain and was eager to retire to a quieter life and marriage. Dorothy Wilson, who was preparing to take over the B.C. School of Dancing, had already joined the staff by the time I went south. The last time I saw "Miss Roper," (by then Mrs. Duncan Crux) I was on a visit home to Vancouver many months later. We met in her Kerrisdale home—she a proud mum with her infant child, Elizabeth.

Pasley Island, my prewar summer paradise.

Pat Ainley. Somewhere between graduating from UBC and heading off to Harvard, he managed to break my heart.

My sister, Leading Coder Moira Sweeny, WRCN.

Waiting for me at home after the war ended were Mum and my naval cadet younger brother Roger, my sister Moira, and my brother Sedley's wife and child. Sedley, shown here, returned later.

The chorus line from Fun For The Money. I had changed my name to Anna Verite.

A publicity shot for The Merry Widow. With another soubrette I snuggle up to Johnny Pelletti.

Dad, taken in 1940, the year of his death.

CHAPTER 3

A Most Difficult Time

I suspect that Bea consulted with June Roper and then with Mum and Dad to bring about my move to Hollywood. I don't remember moving out of the boarding house nor requesting my parents' aid toward further training, but from somewhere my parents, bless them, found the money to send me there. In September 1940, on leave and in uniform, Dad took me and my one suitcase, filled mostly with practice clothes, to the Vancouver bus station. There he kissed me goodbye on the top of my head. Without questioning when I might see him again, I cheerfully boarded the huge Greyhound bus for Los Angeles.

Looking back, I wonder how with him as my parent I could ever have become as self-centred as I was then. I have asked myself whether it was that I hadn't seen enough of him because for years he had been almost completely absent from my life. Or was it because he'd never shared his unhappiness with anyone, and we'd just left him to himself? Why else, I ask myself, would he have returned at that time in his life to the army?

From my front seat on the right-hand side of the bus, I could watch the speedometer. Once out of the city and heading for the border, the bus travelled at great speed, making air-brake noises and swaying its passengers heavily into every curve. The journey continued all night and most of the next day by which time the temperature had risen to over 100 degrees Fahrenheit. With no air-conditioning in the bus, sweat ran off my face and my soggy clothes clung to me as the bus wound its way through the San Fernando Valley. Although the California sky was hidden by what I learned later to call high fog, I could understand why many people wore sunglasses; the glare was unbearable.

From the bus terminal in Los Angeles late in the afternoon, a local bus sped me along bright, wide streets, some edged with palm trees, then along an even wider and brighter freeway ten miles or so to the corner of Sunset Boulevard and La Brea Avenue. There I disembarked. The humidity was less in Hollywood than in the valley, so by that time I had dried off. I walked one block down La Brea Avenue to the Nico Charisse studio.

Situated on the south side of the Chaplin Sound Studios, this dance school must have been the most beautiful in Hollywood. The facade of the low white building, enhanced by four pillars and five broad steps, was set back from La Brea in a landscape of palms and flaming lilies and it was the first time I had ever connected the study of dance with opulence. It gave me the sense of having arrived at an important plateau in my life. Suitcase in hand, I mounted the steps and entered my new world.

Nico Charisse, dark and handsome, an elegant Greek ballet master in his forties, greeted me in the foyer. When I had introduced myself, he showed me a huge studio, empty but for a couple of dancers practising, and led me across it to double doors wide open to the sunshine. From there he pointed to a house on the far side of an old orchard where there were still a few straggly lemon trees.

"That is where you will live, Verity, with nice people called Richardson. Take your grip over and say hello—they are expecting you—and come back right away to my office." As usual, I accepted all that had been arranged for me.

I thanked Nico and picked my way between tufts of dry grass and fallen yellow fruit, maybe a hundred feet to the edge of a trim green lawn. Another few steps and I was at the front door of a charming white bungalow that appeared to be tucked into a high hedge of poinsettia. The scarlet flowers literally dripped into the guttering. Mrs. Richardson welcomed me in an English voice straight from London's Old Vic and I responded quite automatically with a marbles-in-the-mouth "How awfully kaind of you." Her familiar accent seemed an added bonus and augured well for my sojourn there. She showed me to a bright room with white ruffled curtains where I dumped my suitcase, gave her my rent money and accepted her invitation to make myself at home. Then I hurried back across the orchard.

Nico introduced the tall, beautiful woman I had glimpsed behind glass doors when I entered the foyer. "You must meet my wife, Cyd," said Nico, and to his wife, "This is Verity from Canada."

"How do you do?" I greeted her, offering my outstretched hand into which she placed a limp one.

"Pleased ta meecha, ah'm sure."

"Cyd teaches for me," Nico went on "and she's in charge of my office." His wife just smiled. I learned that Cyd was nineteen years old, a former Charisse student and now a star on the rise. Dark-eyed with a lovely, slow smile, she moved like a Southern belle. "She's to be Astaire's dance partner in *Band Wagon*," Nico said proudly. "Her first major role."

I was in awe of these glamorous people, but what struck me most was the casual ease with which they received me as a contemporary. I suppose it was taken for granted that I would go places since June Roper was well-known for her choreography in Ernest Belcher's Hollywood Bowl shows and because earlier Roper students attending the Charisse School had achieved success in their careers. However, recently students had been coming to his studio not so much for what Nico taught, although that was innovative and unique, but because he rented his major practice room to Russia's Bronislav Nijinska (correctly Nijinskaya) who was to be my new teacher. The young Mrs. Charisse was already one of Madam's regular students.

I gave my package of American dollars to Cyd, who wrote me a receipt. My tuition was to begin at eleven the very next day but Cyd told me the studio was always available for warm-up by nine. Then, as

I set off once more to my new home, Nico invited me to watch his class the following afternoon.

The next morning it was easy enough to join the throng in the studio before the lesson—about thirty dancers, each intent on finding a place at the barre, each preoccupied with his or her own practice. But immediately Madam Nijinska entered, the atmosphere changed. I sidled into a corner not to be too visible until I could gauge where I stood as a dancer. At first, anxiety made me tense and awkward, but when I realized that her students were of widely differing strengths, some less well trained than I, my confidence rallied.

Sister of the renowned Vaslav Nijinsky, Bronislav was recognized in the U.S. as the finest classical choreographer on the continent, perhaps in the world at that time. Beginning in 1909, she had danced for five years with the Diaghilev company in Russia. By the age of twenty-three she had choreographed *La Tabatière* in Kiev and soon after had opened her own school there. Her reputation flourished when in 1922 she presented *Renard* and *Les Noces* to music by Stravinsky and went on to create many of the best-known Russian ballets used by all the famous European companies, including the Paris Opera. In 1932 she formed her own company. By 1938 she had moved to the United States and become an American citizen.

At the time I began my classes with her, Madam was forty-nine years old and had been teaching in the United States for a year. She demonstrated mostly with her hands and delicate footwork. The superb carriage of her upper body, her softly rounded, carefully placed arms and her poised head added to the charm of this squarish, quite portly woman whose powerful personality could be felt the moment she entered a room. She spoke English with a very thick Russian accent, relapsing into her own tongue with those who understood.

My first days with her were particularly tough because I couldn't understand her instructions and had to learn her style and idiosyncrasies by following other dancers. The barre exercises were done very slowly—at about half the speed I had become accustomed to at the B.C. Ballet School. This made them doubly difficult; the slower the action the more strength one needs. It felt good for the first few pliés, but before we were halfway through the exercise, my legs had begun to shake. Although I thought I was in good shape and my feet tough, I found myself wet with sweat within minutes. All these exercises were done in pointe shoes and wherever applicable *en pointe*, especially develop-opé which was held in each position for sixteen counts. The first part of the centre practice was a repeat of the entire barre-work only without the support of the barre. After that, Madam indulged us in her own choreography, new every day. I soon adored the work and quickly became confident. Class often continued beyond two hours.

Dancers from visiting ballet companies came to Nico's school to polish their techniques with Madam Nijinska. David Lichine's whole Les Ballets Russes company turned up every day for a week. Even David and his wife, Tatiana Riabouchinska, worked as students. Once I felt secure, not knowing which famous dancer I might find myself fol-lowing—or leading—through an exercise, constantly added thrills and surprises to Madam's vigorous class. Exhausted but satisfied at the end of her lesson, I would run across the orchard to take a shower at my lodging.

The Richardsons were elderly English screen actors who had found a niche in Hollywood as the film industry burgeoned and "talkies" took over from the silent screen. During the thirties, an English accent—real or faked—had been de rigueur for anyone who hoped to make it in the movies, and, as a result, a whole colony of Brits had settled in Hollywood. In 1940, the Richardsons, using their naturally British voic-es, were still managing to live comfortably on their incomes from small parts at the studios, enhanced now and then by a pittance of rent from the likes of me. They were generous and kind, but as the weeks went on, Mrs. Richardson began to see me as undignified because I sat barefoot on her living room floor to sew ribbons on my pointe shoes. My feet weren't pretty. In those days they were, in fact, pretty bloody. When, during class I had asked permission to bandage a heel because of a blis-ter, madam wanted to see the blood through my shoe before excusing me. "To toughen the skin," Nijinska would repeat to all new students.

The endless California summer took some getting used to. The few remaining lemon trees in the lot between the studio and my lodgings were a permanent source of amazement, always in leaf, always in flower, always in fruit. Hollywood, carved out of the desert like the rest of California, depended entirely on underground watering systems to keep lawns green. Lush lawns would quickly return to desert should the water system fail. During the day, the temperature hovered around 112 degrees Fahrenheit, but owing to the very low level of humidity around Hollywood, I didn't suffer from the heat. And since the nights were comparatively cool, I had no problem sleeping once the cricket noises subsided.

Almost as soon as my daily routine had been established, Mrs. Richardson answered a telephone call for me from an American business associate of my Uncle Dick. Byron Carter and his wife Betty had been asked to keep an eye on me. The first time he came to pick me up at the Richardsons', Byron took me for a Saturday lunch at the Biltmore Hotel where dozens of people in street clothes were dancing to a big band in the air-conditioned ballroom! It seemed bizarre to me then to be dancing at noon, but it was only one of Hollywood's many odd customs and a pleasant relief from the heat and glare outside. Although I was usually tired and always penniless, I liked going to the Carters' Santa Monica home on weekends. Betty, who was obviously pregnant, and I had fun shopping, mostly for clothes for the new baby.

Early in my stay in Hollywood, the pain of being spurned by Pat came sharply into focus when a box of yellow roses arrived for me at the Richardsons' house. The card read Pat, nothing else. For a moment my hopes rose. I wanted to get in touch but, responding to a rush of anger and tears, chose to ignore his gesture of friendship and buried my hurt in work.

In my free time, having little spare money, I kept myself busy making my own clothes, cutting the fabrics on Mrs. Richardson's floor. With her help, I even made a tweed coat—too warm for California but, as it turned out, useful later on.

One evening I was called to the telephone to speak to a Mr. Brown who introduced himself as another of Uncle Dick's colleagues. He was the president of Outdoor Advertising Incorporated. Mr. Brown asked if I would be interested in seeing a movie studio. When I explained that as a student I had little free time, he suggested that we might get acquainted over dinner in an authentic Hawaiian restaurant and offered to pick me up the first evening I could spare. Later that week a large black car drew up at my lodging, and out of it stepped a gigantic man wearing an oversized black cowboy hat.

When I opened the door to his knock, Mr. Brown politely removed his hat and shook my outstretched hand. He wore a plain, dark suit with a quiet, narrow tie, and though he must have weighed considerably more than two hundred pounds, he walked gracefully. It felt a bit odd setting off with him but not at all scary.

Not far off Sunset Boulevard he parked and we entered a tropical garden. Following a path banked by bushes and lilies we came upon a quite large, low restaurant almost hidden by palm trees. It had glass on both sides from which one could enjoy views of a magical garden. We were no sooner seated close to a window than there was a rumble of thunder. The well-lit garden went gradually dark and, following several flashes of lightning and more thunder, a patter of rain began to hit the restaurant's tin roof. The rain quickly increased to a cloudburst, overflowing the gutters and splashing down the windowpanes. The storm lasted three or four minutes then, as neatly as it had begun, it ceased! In the garden, lights came on again—fake sunshine—and I could see that only the plants near the window were shining wet. This effective and amusing performance took place once more before Mr. Brown and I finished our fruit-based meal. Before leaving, we browsed through a show of exotic flowers and Hawaiian merchandise; I bought an inexpensive fruit dish carved out of yucca wood and he bought me my first gardenia.

One Saturday afternoon shortly after this, Mr. Brown took me sightseeing around the movie capital. We drove past houses belonging to the stars, not all of them grand, but most of them Spanish-looking, their gardens full of exotic flowers. Then we drove to the Warner

Brothers Studios. Everyone there knew him and treated him with respect. I was amazed at the size of the buildings and sets but saw nothing in production except one small scene that we watched being shot over and over again in a cramped studio. I thought it very boring.

Hollywood movies, I gathered, were not making money at that time. Because of the war, there was no market for American films in Europe and, although they were not actually involved in the war, the American public's attitude toward entertainment had changed. The glamourous, lighthearted movies that had always drawn crowds were flopping miserably. Many of the British stars had returned to Britain to enlist, and hundreds more actors and actresses were out of work. Until the studios started producing tales of wartime heroism and creating encouraging propaganda, they continued to lose money.

The money my parents had given me was just enough to pay my rent and my daily lessons with Nijinska, but I also wanted to take Nico Charisse's late-afternoon class. He agreed to give me lessons in exchange for demonstrating for his junior classes earlier in the afternoon. The class I joined was huge—around twenty students—and I was flattered that from so many available dancers he chose me as his permanent assistant. One evening I was invited to attend a lesson and be one of the ballroom partners for a group of movie people who needed to learn the rhumba for a film. I didn't recognize any of the others, but Nico partnered Bette Davis. He didn't introduce me. Except for her eyes and the odd way she gestured with her chin, she could have been anyone, and since she was not naturally rhythmic, the slinky movement of rhumba proved challenging for her.

For me, this was a fascinating time, meeting and working with show people, and from all the hours of studying and teaching, my own technique was improving rapidly. My future felt assured. I could picture myself taking a lead role, being a success, accepted in my own field of dance as members of my family at home—businessmen and soldiers—were in theirs.

Though I had never worked so blisteringly hard in all my years of training, the toughness of the Russian method, as taught by Nijinska in the morning, was balanced later in the day by the flow of Charisse's technique of spirals which I also loved. Nico would explain the pattern of his balletically-based work by saying, "Divide the body with a continuous line from head to foot and never allow any limb to cross that line." He told us to keep in mind that the line, which extends as far above the head as an arm can reach, can however bend and twist. This meant that the upper body had to twist to the left should the right arm be carried to the left beyond centre front. Therefore the hand of a high arm must not go beyond a line–straight up or curving over–drawn from the top of the head. "The lean or tilt of the head," he said, "determines the limit of the arm movement."

In Nico's technique, attitude grek is a lovely position for an outward pirouette pulled by the top arm into a tight spiral, and the old technical renverse becomes more exotic.

I had been studying in Hollywood for less than three months when, on a Friday in November 1940, Byron called to tell me Betty had delivered a son. He said that after he had seen her and the baby at the hospital he would pick me up and take me to their place for the weekend. When we were driving to his house, he told me he had received a call from my Uncle Dick in Vancouver.

"Your uncle said I should tell you your father won't be coming home."

"Is he going overs..."

Byron interrupted. "Not ever. Your father isn't coming home...ever."

I was unable to speak.

Byron continued, "Your dad died in a military accident. He fell on a sharp instrument that pierced his brain and he never regained consciousness."

Byron drove.

I sat.

In time a deep howl came out of me and I exploded sobbing. I beat the dash board and windows with my fists as I tried to take in what had happened. Then I turned my fury on Byron, shouting, "You're wrong.

It's not my dad. Not him!" But I knew better. Clinging to Byron's arm, I wept uncontrollably.

As soon as he could, Byron left the parkway and stopped the car on a side street waiting for me to compose myself. He held me and tried to dry my face. For a long time I couldn't stop crying.

When I had become silent, Byron drove us to his empty house where he made dinner for the two of us. We ate in silence. The hour was already late and I dearly wanted to be by myself. Familiar with the guest room, I excused myself and slipped away. I didn't cry then, but lying in the dark bedroom a flood of sadness for all the missed chances to tell Dad how I'd loved him came to cover me. I hurt.

Next day at the Carter house, I howled for myself and cried and cried for Mum. Dad's death had come as a powerful shock to my fairy-tale world; until then I had been unaware how much he meant to me. I said to myself, Okay, what should I be doing? Dad's motto had always been "We must push on." Of course, I should be seeing that Mum's all right and then getting on with my own life.

I asked Byron for a some writing paper and a pen. As tears splashed on the writing pad I wrote to Mum all the uplifting things I thought Dad would have said for another person. I knew he believed and trusted in a gentle God who would take care of her.

Shortly after Dad's death, Mum came to Los Angeles and the two of us went to stay with her friend, Dewa Davis, in La Jolla. I found my mother secretive and unusually distant from me. She seemed wrapped in a peculiarly private despair and didn't talk about Dad. I couldn't understand her silence; was there something about Dad's death I wasn't being told?

I adored my father and had learned early to respect and honour him. When I knew him, the principles which forbade him to focus on himself aimed him 100 percent on the welfare of others. This could not always have been so.

The second son of a Vancouver banker, Dad was brought up to appreciate a high standard of living. Although his family was privileged, he was expected to make the most of himself scholastically, artistically and athletically, all of which he did. Yet, when we were growing up, neither he nor Mum ever spoke of his accomplishments.

At the age of twelve, he had been shipped off to Haileybury, the old East India Company school north of London, where, amongst other achievements, he played rugger on the school's First Fifteen in 1907-1908. I don't know if, or how often, he came home to Vancouver in those school years, but that was where his heart lay–by the Pacific Ocean. I do know he was desperately homesick as a school boy and, longing for the beach and the tides, covered his cubicle of a bedroom with pictures of boats, mountains and sunsets. He would have become a sailor had Granny not decided otherwise. She was afraid of the ocean.

So, upon graduation from Haileybury, Dad returned to Canada and entered Royal Military College, Kingston, Ontario, where he achieved the highest honours. As the top cadet in his graduating year (1912) he carried the rank of battalion sergeant major, won the Governor General's Gold Medal for all-round proficiency and the College Sword for best combined high standards in the academic, military and sporting aspects of his training. He was thereby qualified for the one commission in the Royal Engineers at Chatham, England, that was available to a Canadian.

There followed two glamourous pre-First World War years of gentleman soldiering that included every opportunity to shine. His social skills became finely tuned, he was meticulously groomed and perfectly spoken. He played the piano, wrote poetry and spoke French. He also played cricket and rugby and rowed for both the REs and the British Army. He was a natural sailor and a strong swimmer. Between 1913 and 1914 he spent time at the equitation school at Aldershot, and in August of that year was sent to France with the Fifth Cavalry Division of the British Expeditionary Force. He rode in the retreat from Mons and spent the next five years in the thick of conflict.

I never asked and he never told me for what special braveries he had been awarded the Order of the British Empire and Bar, nor why he was twice mentioned in dispatches. He was, despite his background and accomplishments, both a gentle and a shy man.

My mother and father, both born in Vancouver, had grown up as friends. Near the beginning of the First World War, my mother, then Isabel Bell-Irving and engaged to be married to a Canadian soldier, Gerry Heath, had signed on with the Volunteer Aid Detachment (V.A.D) and had followed Gerry and six of her brothers overseas. Working at Lady Riddley's private hospital in London, she'd had occasion to nurse several of her own wounded brothers and it was there in 1916 she'd received the news of Gerry's death. By coincidence, Dad was on leave in London at the time and was there to comfort and care for her. Months later, when he proposed to her, my mother wired to ask her mother's advice.

"Would it be kind or fair for me to marry Ben Sweeny since my heart will always belong to Gerry?" My grandmother's reply read in part, "A woman is lucky to have a man, let alone a kind one."

My parents were married while Dad, having stopped shrapnel with his hands, was on sick leave from France. After a more serious wounding in his hip in 1917, he could have been relieved from active duty and gone home, but in the spring of 1918, while some of his friends still fought in France, he volunteered for the second British and Allied mission in support of White Russian forces fighting the Bolsheviks near Murmansk. Mum took Sedley, their first-born, home to Vancouver to live with her parents.

For another year and a half, Dad commanded a tired and motley British company that was trying to stop the Russian Revolution. Their toughest job was to remain morally and physically strong under defeating conditions that included thin rations and practically no sunlight during the long cold winter. Dad wrote copiously to Mum and sent her programs of the unit concerts arranged by his men to relieve their boredom and the ache to go home. One of the programs Mum received read We Must Push On, by Sweeny. I actually have that fold of yellow paper in my care.

At the end of hostilities, Dad was offered a senior instructor's position with the Royal Engineers in England, but because Mum really wanted him to settle down in Canada, he transferred to the Canadian army and returned home. When Canada's Royal Military College applied to the British War Office for their very best engineer as an instructor, they were given Dad's name. But RMC refused him because he was only a Canadian.

Deeply disappointed, Dad gave up his military career but very soon discovered how challenging it was to make a living as a civilian. Even though various plum jobs such as Safety Engineer to the Port of Vancouver and Chief Engineer of the B.C. Department of Highways came his way, his ignorance of civilian politics and his unbending ideals steered him into conflict with management over poor safety practices and the use of inferior materials. He was let go by the Vancouver Harbours Board when, advised by his Conservative superior to fire his Liberal foreman of works, Dad, though a Conservative himself, had refused because he believed that a man's political persuasion should have nothing to do with building piers.

Another time, when a close friend applied for the same job at the same time as Dad, he turned down the position offered to him "because," he said, "the chap needed it more than I did." For all his effort and perseverance he was not a businessman and fared poorly job-wise all through the long Depression years. It must have seemed obvious to Mum's family, who never seemed to feel the pinch of those years, that we Sweenys were not only poor, but that Dad's honesty was ridiculously naive.

As a loving father he could not have cared more deeply for his children but even when he was working near home, Dad seemed to believe that Mum and the boys could manage without him, and in what might have been his free time, he was forever elsewhere taking care of other more needy people. Devastated by the cruelty of the war, he had joined a group of veterans—Old Contemptibles they called themselves—pledged to assist the families of veterans whose menfolk had been lost or suffered debilitating injuries. Sometimes he took us children with him when he visited a struggling family. He would bring some small thing he knew they needed and, chatting quietly, do his best to give encouragement.

As we grew up, Dad wanted us to understand how much more fortunate we were than children whose families had been shattered by death or wounding or gassing during the war. He tried to explain to us that whatever restrictions our family might have to face from lack of finances, they were nothing compared to the despair with which other families must cope.

While Mum was still visiting in California after Dad's death, the thought struck me that without Dad, she couldn't possibly support any further training for me. Leaving her with Mrs. Davis, I dried my tears and returned to school, but I told my teachers I must find a job. The following week I saw Mum off on the bus to Vancouver and from then on attended every audition posted in the Los Angeles area.

In December I applied to dance in a live musical called *Fun for the Money*. I'd never seen so many dancers auditioning, and some of them appeared to be literally hungry. Only twenty of us got jobs. I had to join the lowest rank of the union known as Chorus Equity. The pay would be minimal. Rehearsals were to begin at 7:00 a.m. on January 3, 1941. Not till then would I have a clue how tough it was going to be to become a chorus girl.

Meanwhile, filled with melancholy thoughts about Dad and very homesick, I'd heard talk of Hollywood's famous Santa Claus Parade and the wonderful Christmas trees lining the route. I decided the parade might cheer me up. Hollywood Boulevard was decorated all right, but there wasn't a Christmas tree in sight—at least, not the kind I knew. Instead, attached back-to-back to each lamp post were a pair of green-painted tin triangles with a few round holes in them. Sandwiched between the triangles and gleaming through the holes, coloured lights represented Christmas balls. Blow-ups of movie stars festooned with tinsel dangled and danced outside the stores, and a mighty parade of actors and actresses dressed in costumes, or lounging in swim suits rode by on huge floats. There were bands that played "Jingle Bells" and there were cowboys and Indians on horses. Although everyone else seemed to be having fun, I couldn't get into the mood of it. Safely back at the Richardsons' house, it warmed my heart to see their small plastic tree, decorated with cotton-wool, icicles and angels. They'd even cut some red poinsettia to grace the dinner table.

Although I had the distinct feeling I didn't belong in this part of the world, with January and my new job rapidly approaching, I spent as many of my last student days as possible at Nico's studio. So eager was I to start supporting myself, on January third, I walked to my first rehearsal at Hollywood Playhouse, the only live theatre on the Boulevard, before the stage door was open. By 7:00, all the girls were on stage. It was easy to tell who was experienced in chorus work because they stood right out in front, while the inexperienced, like me, hung back. The woman in charge quickly sorted us for size and gave us numbers.

Like a repetition of the audition, every girl had to show her kicks and turns, then we followed the director through some basic tap steps before attacking more difficult jazzy moves with complicated rhythms. Although my turns and kicks were as strong as any, I found the up-beat, contemporary steps tricky to learn because they seemed very similar to each other, yet one little mistake threw the whole routine out of sync. I must have looked prissy and overly balletic at first, but by ten o'clock that day the first routine was half set, and I had relaxed and begun to feel more in the groove.

Except for a short lunch break, we worked from early morning until utter exhaustion around 6:00 p.m. every day for two weeks. To get absolute precision, the choreographer repeated each block dozens and dozens of times without a breather between takes. Things like kick-splits and roll-overs were new to me, but Rachael, the one friend I made almost instantly—perhaps because her voice sounded a bit prissy like mine—took pity, showing me some simple tricks.

Following a big publicity barrage, *Fun for the Money* opened to a full house with arc lights criss-crossing the sky. We had spanking new costumes and fresh makeup and there were clear, bright gels in the spotlights. Though I knew little else about the content of the show, I knew what I was doing and thoroughly enjoyed myself. So far, so good. We settled in for a long run.

My new friend Rachael was a pretty girl with dark hair. Because of her voice, I guessed she came from a "nice" (meaning proper) background. Near the end of the first week she told me her boyfriend would be picking her up after the show. He had a friend, she said. Would I like to come along?

"Sure," I said, and after the performance I climbed aboard, the fourth body on the front seat of a pickup truck. The fellow next to me wrapped his arm around me saying, "Well, sweetheart, how's your sex life?" I was nonplussed. I'd been in love, but sex had never even been mentioned. "Sex life?" I said, and laughed, embarrassed. "I have no sex life." And I thought, *How dare you speak to me this way?* I guess I didn't give him the answer he wanted because we just drove around for a few minutes and then they dropped me off at my lodging.

The chorus line in *Fun for the Money* appeared often, danced fast, kicked high, spun like tops and wiggled a lot, but despite endless publicity and an elaborate souvenir program, all those costume fittings and high hopes, the show ran less than three weeks. It was a huge disappointment for me. I remember someone tried to make me feel better by explaining that Hollywood never had been a good town for live shows.

When I went back to school, Nico gave me a trade paper where I read about an audition for a musical review called *Rhapsody in Rhythm* to be presented for the benefit of the British War Relief Association by writer Sara Decoursay. There would be twelve performances at the Ford Bowl, a huge outdoor shell in Balboa Park in San Diego. Two MGM stars, John Elliott and Janice Chambers, had been chosen for leading roles. I turned up at the appointed hour to learn that no chorus girls were required. I didn't rush away, however, and in conversation with a singer learned that the producer was looking for someone to direct stage movement for the singers and actors. Mrs. Decoursay agreed to see me and I told her about my training and the choreographic scholarship I had received from the Royal Academy. Not only was I given the job of stage choreographer, Mrs. D. also mentioned two short spots that could use dance solos and invited me to prepare some appropriate material after I had read the script. For one of my solos I adapted a tap number that had won me a first place in a British dance competition. The other, which was minuscule, filled a bridge between choruses of a love duet sung by the stars. Neither was classical, but this show of confidence from Mrs. Decoursay gave me just the impetus I needed to make another change I had contemplated for some time. In those days classical dancers took on European professional names, and I had already decided that Sweeny was inappropriate. From then on I called myself Anna Verite.

Although the cast was predominantly white, Mrs. Decoursay and her staff were black. I was struck by the gentleness of their manners and their quiet way of putting together this elaborate show accompanied by a symphony-and-swing band conducted by Herb Wilkins. As for choreography, I focused on clean and dramatic entrances and exits, made suggestions for some extensive movement to fill the very large stage and helped group and regroup the singers, who were accustomed to performing without any action. There was no doubt I earned my very small salary. All the performances of this review-type musical were well received, but I remember how odd it felt to be dancing in a spotlight out-of-doors with a still-bright sky overhead. Like my new name, this was a new experience for me.

That spring the annual two-week California downpour was so heavy it flooded the streets of Hollywood and brought down sand by the ton from the Hollywood Hills. I was at Nico's school when the storm first broke and can still picture the Charisses, barefoot in summer clothes, carrying a card table by the legs over their heads to keep off the pelting rain. Rushing to put the top up on their convertible, they found it already half-full of water! As there was no street drainage system to carry water away, puddles developed everywhere. One day I plunged from the bus into a lake outside the Bon Marche. Most people knew enough to wear sandals which let the warm water come and go easily.

Californians used snowploughs to clear away the sand. Outside the town, the rain flushed citrus fruit from orchards onto the roads and into overflowing ditches. The waste seemed appalling; I wanted to gather sacks-full of grapefruit. Almost instantly I noticed a change in the colour of the natural foliage. Grass, that had lain dead and bleached from June through February now sprouted at high speed, covering every bare spot on the hills and it was soon knee-high along the highways.

Thanks to Nico again, I was hired in April by Arthur Spitz as lead-line dancer and soloist for his new Light Opera Company based at the Mason Theatre in Los Angeles, a long bus-ride from Hollywood. At the first rehearsal I met Barbara Ward, a singer from the San Francisco Opera Company. We became friends and soon decided to share a small apartment in LA.

The first production was *Rose Marie*, with music by Rudolph Friml and Herbert Stothart, book by Otto Harbach and Oscar Hammerstein II. Although the star seemed a bit old for the role, Virginia Card had a thrilling voice and Elm Halprin made a dashing Mountie. All very "Western," there were Indians, frontier barmaids and night-club dancers. The dance chorus were mini-skirted cowgirls.

For my first solo in a scene from the second act set in a gown shop in New York, I arranged a balletic Highland fling. To accompany me, conductor Fritz Berens managed to create an amazing likeness to the sound of bagpipes even though he had only the smallest of concert orchestras. My very first press clipping was a rave review. The headline read Nightly Curtain Calls for a Highland Lass. I even received extravagant flowers at the stage door. The sender left his card but, although I was intrigued, I hadn't the nerve to follow instructions to his promised rendezvous. I remember how torn I was then, and how I later tried to imagine how different my life might have been if I'd had the courage to investigate.

For the rest of that spring and early summer my life was a whirl of rehearsals, costume fittings, photographs and opening and closing nights as we moved from *Rose Marie* to *The Merry Widow*. I learned more than I expected, but what I learned had little to do with dance.

Backstage at the Mason Theatre, I began to recognize that the cast was not a happy family. The comedy team of Pelletti and Westerfield got along all right, but the women in the cast were all fighting over them. James Westerfield, who did well in movies later on, though an enormous man, was said to be a good lover. John Pelletti, lean, dark and beautiful, played straight man to his clown. Johnny was the girls' sex idol. Betty, the dancer next to me at the makeup table, said she had slept with him one night but the next day he wouldn't speak to her. She was an aspirin junkie, and went on benders. She was also voluptuous and loved entertaining the other dancers in the dressing room by using her greasy black eyebrow pencil to draw a pig's snout around each of her nipples and making up lewd conversations between her breasts as she flopped them about. No one but I seemed the least embarrassed by these performances.

I found the boys in the theatre orchestra less bewildering than the stage performers. Once, after a midnight dinner I went along with Jim, a quiet saxophonist, to one of their hotel rooms which had two big beds with enough room for several people in each. Like the half-dressed couples in the other bed, I found myself sitting up in bed beside Jim. He seemed to feel as awkward as I, uncertain why he was there. It became obvious we didn't belong and we left. The rest stayed all night, I guess. I wasn't invited again. Jim drove me up the coast to see the sun come up over Santa Paula.

Prissy Anna Verite continued to be shocked and bewildered. "They're at it again!" a stagehand warned, laughing, as he jerked his thumb in the direction of the darkened backstage. "Maisie's in there necking with Mitzy's guy!" I couldn't laugh about it.

Theatre life, in Los Angeles anyway, seemed one long series of affairs. Members of the cast were jealous and gossipy. They started rumours and told outright lies about each other. At the same time they kept their eyes open for any opportunity. "You're a fool if you don't grab it when it comes," I heard one person advising another. "Go ahead and take the guy! They're all fair game, you know!"

It seemed to me that gullible fame seekers loved and bought these ideas and swallowed them whole. It also seemed that there was no limit to the depth these people would stoop to to get what they wanted. It was common knowledge that everyone who went for an audition at

Earl Carrol's famous theatre restaurant would be asked, "Do you or don't you? If you don't, you can leave right now." It was ironic that carved above the fancy entrance gate to his establishment was the slogan, Through These Portals Pass the Most Beautiful Girls in the World. It should have also added, and They're Available as Bed Partners. Fortunately, I didn't qualify to work at Earl Carrol's for another reason; they only wanted tall showgirls.

Nothing I had pictured about theatrical success or being loved or getting married was true here. Either my dreams were false or these people were. Not only did everyone play around with sex, making it grubby, exposed and unattractive, but they flaunted it, laughed at it and used it vengefully. No one seemed to care that in Hollywood morals had gone by the board. No one said "Behave yourselves!" Even the authorities, management and the police, seemed not to notice. Although I felt jealous of the people of my age who seemed to enjoy this life without limitation, without curbs or policing, I didn't understand the cruel games they played. In time I became resentful.

No one seemed to mind making their private lives public. It was all good publicity. Everywhere I went I noticed people's desperate effort to be seen and recognized. They seemed to be all shine and sparkle on the surface. But I was surprised how often only a thin layer of self-assurance protected a frightened personality battling for position and money. Eventually it dawned on me that behind the scenes it was a scared lot of humans who fought for a place in the sun or a picture in a magazine or to be seen with someone even more important than they thought themselves.

Bewildered, I floated through the Hollywood show business world wearing my false eyelashes and dancing the Merry Widow Waltz, unseen, barely communicating. It never dawned on me that it was I who didn't fit. Somehow, except for my naive romance with Jim, I escaped heartbreak.

None of my jobs paid much. None of them lasted long. During the third production with the Mason Light Opera Company, someone looted the box-office receipts and the company threatened to fold. To drum up business and keep the show going, the cast responded by riding around LA and Hollywood in costume on top of a hay-wagon. If I heard "The show must go on!" once, I heard it a dozen times, but I'd had enough. I wrote home, and in late July, Bea Abercrombie came to my rescue once again with an ad cut from a Vancouver newspaper. Wanted: experienced ballet teacher with broad background. Constance Hart School of Dance, Seattle, Washington. Within a week I had received a job offer that was considerably closer to home.

Anna Verite, the new ballet mistress at the Constance Hart School of Dance in Seattle.

CHAPTER 4

The Constance Hart School of Dance, Seattle

My letter of application to teach at the Constance Hart School of Dance was answered jointly by Miss Hart and her sister, Lily H. Johnson. Constance accepted me as ballet mistress in her school and her sister offered me room and board in her house for a very reasonable price; because of the minimal teaching fee I had agreed to, this was most welcome.

One Saturday in September 1941, after an overnight bus journey from Los Angeles, I was met at the Greyhound depot in Seattle by Lily Johnson. I was still getting used to my newly acquired stage name, and so I accidentally introduced myself as Verity Sweeny. Lily's warm greeting, delivered in a strong southern drawl, delighted me. When I called her Mrs. Johnson, she said, "Yew're Verdee, Ah'm Lily. Okay?"

Lily wasn't young, and though several inches taller than I, she couldn't have weighed more than 115 pounds. Delicately freckled, her translucent complexion contrasted with the bright lipstick she wore, emphasizing the bits of gold bridgework showing among her teeth.

On arrival at her home, a rambling frame place that perched on the side of a hill, she showed me my bedroom and the bathroom I would use on the second floor. From this level I could catch a glimpse of Lake Washington. Downstairs Lily showed me the kitchen, the sitting and dining rooms—both dark and sombrely furnished—and the equally dark parlour in which sat a very old woman. Lily introduced her mother, Beatrice Hart.

Later in the afternoon, I was upstairs in my room unpacking when Lily called up the stairs, "Yoo hoo, Verdee, will y'all join me for a cup a corfee?"

I followed the aroma to her kitchen. Now that Lily had removed her trim black coat, I saw that although her print dress hung loosely on bony shoulders, she had an elegant carriage and I quickly learned she was less frail than she appeared. Lily began by telling me that, following her husband's death in Louisville, Kentucky, she had come home to Seattle. With her inheritance she had bought this house for herself and her son Claude, but it also had bedrooms for her widowed mother, two of her brothers and two sisters. Claude, she said, was a postgraduate student at the University of Washington. Her sister Constance Hart, a musician, ran the ballet school. Another sister, Elizabeth, a seamstress, made gold-embroidered pocket insignia at a factory; her brothers Tom and Jim Hart were both railwaymen. Lily explained that they all came home for dinner and to sleep, but she didn't say whether she charged them rent. I learned that it was Lily who shopped for groceries, who paid the light and telephone bills and made all the meals. I supposed she must be paying for Claude's education, and began to suspect that she had set Constance up in her school. I was amazed when Lily told me she also held a responsible, full-time job at the Seattle Port Authority.

Still in my rumpled travelling clothes, I was sitting on a stool listening to Lily when Claude entered from the back porch and threw his briefcase on a counter. A gangly six-foot-four with salt-and-pepper hair thinning at the temples, he seemed all Adam's apple and neck. On the ends of his very long arms hung the longest hands I'd ever seen. I glanced down at his huge feet, then my eyes went back up to really look at him. He had a lean and angular face with unusually full lips that could easily cover his large protruding teeth. Like his mother, his gold dental work showed.

"Come in, son, come in heah. Verdee, le'me introduce mah son, Claude." (Lily said it more like *cloud*). "He's a mighty fine dancer, but he's gonna be a professah first."

I jumped off my perch. "How do you do?" I said, sticking out my hand and suddenly feeling very small. My hand was lost in his. Looking up, I saw his huge grin.

"Ah'm doin' jes' fine, thank you, ma'am. Pleased t'make yo aquaintance." Claude turned to his mother, "This the new dance teacher, the Canadian from California?"

"Right you are, son, and a most interestin' lady, t'be sure. Ah'm jes' dyin' t'see her dance."

"Y'all do any ballroom dancin'?"

"Yes, I love it. I learned the Sylvester method. Do you know it?"

"What method did y'all say?"

"Victor Sylvester. You must have heard of him." I looked at Lily who was looking adoringly at her son. I could tell they were close, though they didn't hug or kiss.

I was back in my room when Constance Hart arrived home and Lily called me down again. In the living room, a large woman of middle age turned to face me extending her hand. "I'm Constance Hart and you must be Anna." I was jolted, not only because no one in California had recognized me by my new name, but also because of Miss Hart's appearance. Her face, covered by a thick white paste trying to hide a rough skin condition, was made up like a painted doll with large pink circles on her cheekbones. Her brows were dark against the stark white, and dark lashes circled the bluest of eyes.

"Welcome to Seattle," she said. I was still transfixed, noticing how her mass of jet-black hair, pulled fiercely away from a centre part was fashioned into two long braids that crossed at the back of her head and came forward again to make circles over her ears. "You may call me Constance at home." She spoke with precision, scarlet lips emphasizing her startlingly white teeth. Why didn't Constance have a southern drawl? I wondered. Friendly enough but business-like, she continued, "I expect you to call me Miss Hart at school." This came as no surprise to me. In fact, I welcomed it. I had found the American habit of using first names quite uncomfortable after my years in England. Miss Hart was one of the few people who made a serious effort to call me Anna. She said the students would use Miss Verite.

When Lily had brought her sister a cup of coffee, we sat in the over-stuffed chairs to discuss my journey. Niceties quickly over, Miss Hart said she had spent the day taking registrations at the school. She hoped I was prepared for a busy season. Most of the classes, she said, were booked to capacity. I noticed that Miss Hart's hands, which she used expressively, were small and white and that her fingernails were scarlet. On one of her small fingers she wore a sizable sapphire.

I later learned from Lily that, when she was young, Miss Hart had become an accomplished pianist, had played professionally and had been much in demand as an accompanist for singers. She had also sung and coached singers. Although no one ever explained it to me, I suspected something very sad had thwarted that career, and guessed it had something to do with her scarred face.

The Constance Hart School had been established for over ten years and had recently blossomed under the instruction of an excellent young ballet dancer by the name of Lee Foley who had been trained in the only Seattle school Miss Hart looked upon as competition. Lee's sudden departure for the Metropolitan Opera Ballet in New York was the reason I had been hired. When I heard about his impressive local reputation, it provided a good challenge for me. Lee later earned star status and danced lead roles at the Metropolitan.

On various occasions when I had been sent on teaching assignments at suburban ballet schools in England, I had been disappointed by the quality of students. However, the students I met at Miss Hart's school were a real eye-opener. Even the youngest was polite and tidily dressed. Following introductions by Miss Hart, each group, without direction, took places at the barre. Since they'd had firm grounding, these students literally had no bad habits to overcome. My predecessor must have held them in his hand. They seemed quite unspoiled. There were no stragglers. It soon became obvious that my dance language was similar to Lee's; by the time I had described to Miss Hart with my voice and hands the length and tempo of an exercise, the students already understood what I wanted. Although she used no sheet music, when Miss Hart played the piano her improvisation matched every exercise perfectly.

During the afternoons, I taught as many as four hours of children's classes as well as private lessons. For the first few weeks I stuck to basics, but, since I was not bound to teach any particular method, such as Royal Academy or Cecchetti, I gradually felt free to focus on heads and arms and to extend the exercises my own way for the sheer joy of it. At all levels of performance the children were keen to learn and although several had almost insurmountable foot problems and couldn't consider pointe-work, whatever we did was joyful because of the music.

The professional class, a group of nine, not all of whom came daily, was the most interesting to teach. Ready each morning at eleven, they dressed in an odd assortment of balletic gear. I worked along with them and was often challenged by them. Miss Hart's accompaniment would have given anyone encouragement. She felt and played every nuance of every move we made.

Using parts of the many variations on barre-work I had learned in England and with June Roper, with Madam Nijinska, and with Nico Charisse, I created several of my own syllabi, adding arm and body movements that made the exercises particularly alive. After working up a real sweat—splashing the walls and soaking our towels—we approached the long, slow exercises that needed most control. I believe I was able to bring more exuberance to my teaching than these students had experienced before. They seemed to enjoy our times together. I would throw at them all the most difficult enchainements of batterie and elevation I could devise and they would stick with me until we perfected them. I am sure at least one or two went on to professional careers.

I'm ashamed to say I took Miss Hart's fine accompaniment quite for granted, but she appeared to enjoy the richness that her music added to the quality of my teaching and seemed perfectly happy to complement my dance skills. She knew music and I knew dance. We got along well and grew together as a teaching team, both of us having trained in the old-fashioned school of hard work.

I didn't look forward to Saturdays, which were often twelve-hour days. Several completely different groups came to take musical-comedy, tap, jazz and social dancing, all of which I was trained to teach but none of which enthralled me.

However, Miss Hart seemed delighted with the students' progress and before long suggested I choreograph dances for myself to gems from her repertoire. From then on, she made time for us to work together on *my* dance career in *her* studio! She often arrived at the studio ahead of me, not only to do the office work and sweep and dust, but to practice piano and to sing lovely, gentle, emotional songs. She didn't seem to mind my listening as I prepared for the incoming class. Later she suggested I should sing and offered to coach me. My voice, she said, was a clear soprano and unwobbly. She also said I had perfect pitch. Occasionally, when I am sad, I still recall and sing songs that she taught me. This much I remember of one that I loved.

"Let it be beautiful when I sing the last song.
I will have the sun to shine upon my body.
I will have the wind to play upon my body.
The whole world will I have,
To make music for me.
Let it be beautiful when I sing the last song.
Let it be day..."

Back at the house after a day's work at the school Miss Hart went straight to her room. That was when Lily bombarded me with politics as she and I prepared dinner in the kitchen. From her I learned what little I knew of what was going on in the world. Although I wasn't familiar with the American situation, I reacted sharply—"Hey! Don't forget I'm Canadian!"—to Lily's anti-British sentiments and her bitterness that Britain still owed the United States millions of dollars for American help in the First World War. "No way," said she, "is the USA going to get involved in another fracas over there!" Still, she said she loved me and even hinted she'd be pleased to have me for a daughter-in-law.

Claude expected to get his doctorate in languages—"English, with French on the side," was how he put it. My own interest in literature, fostered by Pat, sparked my willingness to help Claude study and brought us together, and as time went on we became good friends. His voice was deep, almost gargley, and though his speech was coloured by his southern upbringing, I was fascinated that he used words and phrases culled from the English literature he was studying. I enjoyed being with him and he with me. He had fixed up part of the basement as a music room, a place where he could bring his university friends. With them he sometimes spoke French. Claude had a set of drums and other percussion gadgets such as maracas, claves and a cow-bell. Whenever his friends brought instruments, they'd have a jam session.

Since Lily's house was built on a hillside, from that basement room at the back of the house one could look out toward the lake. There of a Sunday, Claude and I would sit on cushions on the floor with our backs propped against an old chesterfield and Claude's long legs reaching well into the room. Grammar books and French studies surrounded us; I held the book and asked questions while he memorized. After we had worked a while, we often sat close holding hands, listening to his records. When one day he put his arm around my shoulders, I enjoyed the safe, warm feeling of being enveloped.

Claude was not like those Hollywood men I'd met. He respected me and I trusted him. We got along well because he loved jazz, and I was keen to know more about it. He also danced with a lot of style. Actually, he tap-danced and in his loose-limbed fashion reminded me very much of the Nicholas Brothers, an American duo I had seen several times in London with Blackbird Reviews. Both his tallness and his six extra years appealed to me. Although I belittled his slouch and rumpledness, something about his ease of movement—how he flipped his ankles and wrists and let the weight of his long limbs swing themselves—was enormously attractive to me. He seemed a bit puppet-ish, but never with the strings pulled tight.

Sometimes Claude invited me to go with him to friends' houses where students gathered and we danced and sang. Although we must have looked odd dancing together, it quickly became obvious that Claude and I made a good team. Mutt and Jeff, we created routines and performed them for all Claude's friends. We laughed and had great fun dancing together, holding strongly and whirling about until we both dripped with sweat, hugging madly at the end so as not to crash, with everyone clapping and screaming. Claude's sense of timing was infectious. He moved so well that I was able to relax and let him lead. Then we tried jazz and tap-dancing together. I knew all the steps but I had never felt so completely at home with the rhythms.

One night in Lily's car coming home from such a party Claude told me that some day he would marry me. He insisted he was serious and asked me to wear a ring he had been given by his grandmother. In fact, it was her wide gold wedding band, which he wore on his little finger. Although I was touched and flattered, I declined. But Claude persisted and would have me try it on my third finger. It fit. Although I knew I shouldn't, despite my guilt about letting myself enjoy this close friendship, I didn't know how to say no. I agreed to wear the ring, comforting myself with the thought that no one who mattered would ever see it. I had never said "I love you." I would give it back very soon.

But I didn't. It felt grown-up to wear a ring; I liked the look of it, liked the feeling of being promised to someone and began to look at Claude differently. I let him kiss me; let him put his arm around me in front of his mother. Lily lent me her diamond engagement ring to see how it felt on my finger. Things were changing, but our relationship still didn't feel right. I felt that neither Claude nor his family were in my class. I had been brought up to believe in a class structure where my family, and others like them, held superior positions to other people. I told myself Claude's interest in show-business—a facet of my life that had sometimes been used by others to embarrass me—was to blame for our relationship, nothing more. But I couldn't tell him that.

I felt pangs of guilt that I was letting myself get too close to him because I knew our partnership could never be permanent if for no other reason than that I couldn't imagine becoming a member of Lily's family. Except for Claude and Lily and me, there was next to no conversation when we gathered around the dinner table. Miss Hart seldom spoke at all. "Pass the gravy, Joe," Tom might say. "Seen the new light at First and Pine?" Joe asked everyone. "Traffic's gettin' heavier every day downtown." After they'd cleaned their plates, Tom and Joe retired to their basement rooms. Constance disappeared to her room upstairs. Elizabeth looked after her mother's dinner tray, then helped clear the table and joined Lily and Claude and me in the kitchen. Not only did I find these people terribly depressing, I also doubted the value of my friendship with Claude; since I didn't consider him my equal, I knew I didn't belong with him, nor he with me.

During my studies in England, I'd had to find my way with little guidance, and being alone in California I should have grown wiser. But I obviously hadn't. When Easter holidays came, I chose not to listen to my doubts and invited Claude to travel north with me to B.C. to spend a weekend at our family cottage on Pasley Island.

Although by 1942 Pasley's unspoken protocol of no politically or racially unacceptable guests appeared to be wearing thin, since Claude was American, loved raucous jazz, didn't swim or sail, wasn't handsome and had no money, I don't know why I risked taking him home. It must have been a hurtful streak in me that wanted to impress by showing him the environment in which I felt I really belonged. It may also have been because I wanted to shock my Victorian mother by daring to flaunt my grown-up independence. I should have remembered how cruel she could be.

The weather that Easter was lovely, and so was the journey from Seattle by bus. From the Vancouver terminal, we took a cab to the water-taxi that whisked us westward out of the harbour. It was only then that I remembered the wedding ring still on my hand. I had intended to leave it in Seattle. Instinctively I covered it with my right hand. I couldn't let Claude see me remove it now.

When we docked at Pasley, I introduced Claude to Mum awkwardly but with enthusiasm. I was embarrassed now because I realized what I had done was dumb, and I deliberately whisked Claude away, chattering that I must show him my special haunts from childhood. I knew that had I taken him directly to Mum's house, she would have looked from one to the other of us and plainly registered her disapproval.

As Claude and I left the meadow, I excused myself and detoured to an outdoor biffy where I removed the ring, tucked it into the breast-pocket of my shirt and buttoned it shut. Claude and I followed trails and scrambled up overgrown mini-mountains as I searched out secret places from years gone by. An hour or so later when we showed up for a meal, Mum was cool but not impolite. She told us she'd heard there was to be a gathering at the old caretaker's house after dinner, and word had been passed to bring music and a cushion. I asked if she would come. To my surprise, she agreed.

Suddenly I remembered the hidden ring and felt for it. The ring was not in my pocket. Though I didn't say a word to Claude, my mind raced. On what rough bit of trail might it have dropped out? When we were climbing over those fallen trees? When we slid down the mossy rocks at South Bay? I would retrace our steps early, early the next morning before Claude was awake.

Freddy Preston was at the party with his guitar and a couple of others had percussion instruments. While most of us sat on the floor, Mum, who was not usually a party person, joined the older people who sat on chairs. Someone had a record player and several current recordings. Before long all the young people were jiving. Before much longer Claude and I began one of our routines with the usual effect—everyone else stopped dancing to watch. I don't recall that we'd had any alcohol but I never needed it. Dancing made me high and I danced with great confidence though I was aware this wasn't the kind of ladylike dancing my mother would have expected of me. However, I stayed close beside Claude and kept up with his every sensual twist and sexy gesture, which certainly seemed to delight everyone who watched. Everyone, that is, except my mother who in one mighty swoop dragged me from the floor by a handful of my hair.

"Verity, how could you?" was all she said. But her face told of her disgust. I covered my embarrassment with laughter, loudly scolding my old-fashioned mother.

The other young people responded with "Oh, Aunt Iso, don't stop them!" and "Please, we're having such a good time." But the atmosphere of fun had been dissipated. Mother's bucket of cold water finished the party. Next morning I crept out early to search for the ring. I couldn't find it.

That weekend cost me most of my new self-assurance. I slunk back to Seattle, trying to explain to Claude on the bus what it had all been about, something he probably understood better than I. Claude never asked what became of the ring. Neither did I tell him what happened to it. Not knowing how to apologise, from then on I avoided him and we went our different ways.

With the end-of-term concert only six weeks away, Miss Hart and I got to work in earnest. Most of the dances had been set, but there was much polishing still ahead. I had designed the costumes and sent the plans and fabrics home with the children but I wasn't content with some of the mothers' sewing and took on a lot of the corrections myself.

I planned to dance a Chopin nocturne created by me with Miss Hart's accompaniment, but the only time for making my own costume was late at night when I should have been sleeping. I was already working beyond my capacity and there came a time during rehearsal when, from sheer tiredness, my eyes failed. It was as if half of each eye had been blacked out, and what was left of my vision was strung with blinking Christmas lights. I got myself a chair and for the first time instructed from a sitting position. It scared me; but I didn't tell Miss Hart what was wrong.

With Constance Hart at a grand piano in the pit, the performance went extremely well, except that I jumped on the lighting-man for missing cues—I had prepared a plot that was far too complicated to handle without hours of rehearsal. Anyway, I guess the stage crew carried the whole thing without my help.

At the close of the concert the applause was wonderful. I sent the groups out, one after the other as we had practised, and then took a bow as choreographer. But they still went on clapping. I went back for another bow and then brought the students in again. It wasn't until I was out there for the third time that I noticed a spotlight shining down on Miss Hart and it dawned on me that I should have recognized her. Stupidly unaware of her position, not only as head of the school but, more importantly for me, provider of the vital music component, I had ignored her. There was nowhere to hide. Lily put me straight next day without sparing my feelings. But I had offended Miss Hart and though I apologised, I was not forgiven.

Accompaniment had always been something we took for granted in schools in England. It was customary for the school's top pianist to attend major examinations and to provide support at competitions without acknowledgement. But this was no excuse. Never again would I take music or the person who played it for me for granted. I was duly chastised. A feeling of shame settled in my diaphragm causing it to ache. Perhaps I had become too sure of myself. But although I had acknowledged my faux pas and apologised, Miss Hart dismissed anything good I had so far accomplished. Thankfully, only a few weeks of summer school remained before I could go home for August. I wished I could just leave and never come back, but though I had no contract, I did have an obligation. Since I hadn't been fired nor had I asked Miss Hart to give me my leave, I knew I was expected to teach again in the fall.

I was thankful that Mum never mentioned the Claude episode when I returned to spend the summer at Pasley; I presume she felt she had fixed that. But when in September I returned to Seattle I could tell by Miss Hart's cold glance I was in for trouble. Working with her was tense and difficult. She played exactly what was necessary for classes, not a single note more, and answered my questions abruptly.

My faux pas further affected my already strained relationship with Lily and Claude. However, I was not beholden to Claude for my social life by this time as a connection from Vancouver had introduced me to Ken, a British naval officer. Ken's minesweeper, HMS *BYMS-10*–one of 150 yard minesweepers produced in the United States for Britain and serving in the Pacific–had struggled back for repairs into the Seattle dockyard where she had been built. Ken and I saw each other quite often, and as a result I sometimes came in late to my boarding house. Perhaps my work suffered. But when Miss Hart called me insolent and rude and began to interfere with my personal life, telling me when and with whom I could go out, I brooded and became angry. When she opened my letters, we fought. Never before had I spoken to anyone with such fury.

Seattle was not the place I wished to be, and as soon as it was possible, I got on a Vancouver bus to spend a couple of days at home. It was on that weekend–more than two years after my father's death–that I learned through innocent conversation with my cousin Con, how cruelly word of his death had come to my mother. The telegram, delivered to her by hand from Canadian military headquarters, had stated that Major S.F.C. Sweeny had been killed in an accident at Camp Debert. It also said that he fell on a sharp instrument which had pierced his brain and that he never regained consciousness. These facts were not new to me, but Con continued that to add to my mother's shock, the telegram had also announced that since Major Sweeny had not yet proceeded overseas, his wife was ineligible for an army pension. This I had not heard. Neither had anyone explained to me until Con did, that for those who understood military jargon, the precise description of his death indicated that Dad had committed suicide. I had not considered this and couldn't accept it. In my view, an honourable man could not commit such an act of cowardice and bring disgrace upon his family. My father was the most honourable of men.

Then it occurred to me that if what Con had said were true, it would explain my mother's unwillingness to speak to me of Dad's death. Con remembered that her own father had left for Ottawa immediately to ensure that my dad was given a proper funeral with military honours, and to secure some sort of pension for Mum, both of which he had been able to arrange. But I had not been told the truth. Nor, I later learned, had my sister or younger brother. Confused and saddened, I returned to Seattle.

Shortly after my return I was shaken by an unexpected message from Norman Silk, a lad who had been my friend in London during the thirties. We had corresponded for a while following my return to Canada in 1938. His warm and humorous letters had touched me but, while I knew that he felt strongly about our relationship, hoping that it would flourish, I had treated his ardour lightly. I told him I thought he was mad to gather food coupons in England to send Black Magic chocolates all the way to Canada for my birthday. He had stopped writing after he was transferred from a regiment of the London Scottish to the RAF and his posting abroad was imminent. By the autumn of 1942, more than two years had passed since we had exchanged letters.

When I arrived home from the studio that evening, Lily pointed out two odd-looking printed sheets on the hall table. They had come in the mail and were addressed to me. About six inches square, these copies of hand-written pages, dark and difficult to read, were called airgraphs, a form that was issued in Britain for letter-writing during the Second World War. Censored, then photographed in reduced size, each single sheet travelled separately. Between Britain and her colonies the service was quite speedy but not so to other countries. From India to the United States, delivery could take three or four months, and messages did not necessarily arrive in sequence. The Americans eventually produced aerograms but there was no cooperation between the postal systems.

Norman had written from a hospital in Calcutta. One page described the wretched climate and from the other I gathered he had been terribly ill. I was filled with guilt about the way I had casually dismissed him, and I replied to these pieces of letters immediately. Because I had lived through several emotional traumas of my own and still suffered humiliation over Miss Hart's attitude, I could now better understand Norman's emotions and feel some of his pain.

In the course of the next few weeks I received many more of Norman's pages, re-directed to Seattle from Vancouver by my Uncle

Dick. I learned that his illness had been diagnosed as rheumatoid arthritis and that he had been almost completely crippled by it. This I explained to Miss Hart who, though still distant with me, seemed to have some empathy for Norman.

Despite the confusion and frustration caused by postal delays, through the exchange of dozens of minute pages and my letters, Norman and I re-examined for each other the past three years of our lives. Because we had so much to talk about we often wrote many pages at a time, and with the postal system so unpredictable it was essential he address each airgraph page separately and number it. Only rarely did a whole sequence from Norman arrive at the same time. The following is from an airgraph which had taken many months to reach Seattle:

Flt./Lt. N.B. Silk
274 Wing R.A.F
Calcutta, India
September, 1942

I'm getting better, Sweeny. I can use my fingers and walk again. When transportation becomes available they still plan to ship me home and discharge me, but while in India I retain the privileges, thin as hospital privileges are, of my RAF commission and pay. One of the most welcome and valuable things my brother Col has sent from home is my [bagpipe] chanter; from the moment I started seriously using my lungs and pressing my fingers over the stops, things began to improve. When at my request the orderlies carried me up the mountain and dumped me into one of the hot pools—even before I could move my body enough to swim—I could float on my back and, blowing into the pipe, begin to get notes again. It amused me to speculate what the vultures, circling low against the hot blue sky, thought of my croaking.

Don't, for God's sake, ever get rheumatoid arthritis.

It has been a very long time, Sweeny, since seeing a letter from you made my heart thump. I don't even know if

you got my last effort, pretty scratchy, no doubt bloody difficult to read, addressed to you c\o Mrs. Sweeny, North
Lonsdale p.o., B.C., by a fellow officer. I wonder where you
are.

Without telling anyone, I had devised a plan to escape from Seattle and the Harts. I decided to work on my technique so as to be ready to audition for the first touring ballet company to come to that city in early spring. Having made my decision, I began letting myself into the studio at seven in the morning to practise alone for three or more hours. Even though the situation between Miss Hart and me was still emotionally painful and was deepened by the unanswered questions about Dad's death, my new goal kept me going.

I had always been an eager student, but that autumn I worked more diligently than ever before. The results astonished me. As I practised with infinite care and stuck to the things that had been difficult for me, they became easy. I never took a short cut and never faked anything. As a result, my pointe-work became strong and fast. I could bourrée like lightning wherever I pleased. The more I stretched, the further my limbs extended. I repeated pirouettes until threes and fours and fives were nothing, and my balance remained secure. It was amazing how quickly I improved now that my focus had become clear. As my mus-cles grew stronger, leaving the ground became effortless, while land-ings were sure but soft. I lost weight on a careful diet monitored by the local drugstore's weighing machine, which gave me back my penny each time I guessed correctly (half a pound per day). I had no food phobia, just a huge desire to perfect my work and get out of Seattle.

I wrote myself a résumé, rewrote it many times, and gradually began to feel confident about the attributes I gave myself. I also began writ-ing letters of application. I felt a quiet satisfaction that at last I really knew what I wanted and that I was doing the right things to get me to where I should go.

Among the résumés I sent out was one to Britain's Alicia Markova, recognized world-wide at that time as prima ballerina of the American Ballet Theatre. Another had gone to her equally famous dance partner,

Anton Dolin, also British. I felt familiar with these important dancers because they had been part of my student life in England. Since about age thirteen I had joined the crowds backstage who begged their autographs.

One morning, before Miss Hart arrived at the studio to investigate it, the envelope I most wanted was delivered there. Written in the giant swirls of Miss Markova's elegant script, the letter indicated that she would be pleased to audition me in February when the company was to have six performances in Seattle at the Civic Auditorium. She included the company's schedule for the next few months and asked me to keep in touch.

I still didn't tell Miss Hart. I didn't know how to tell her. But one day, after a nasty spat over the way she was behaving toward me, I said flatly that I would leave. "And what's more," I said testily, "I have somewhere to go. Markova says she will see me." Except for my occasional angry outburst, we still didn't talk after that but although this didn't make us better friends, I think she had a new respect for me.

After Ken's ship returned to war duty in the Pacific, I felt terribly isolated. I kept the two much-censored letters he wrote and still have his photo in a locket. The little ship did indeed survive the war–I hope with her crew intact. As part of the U.S. lend-lease program she was later turned over to the American navy.

More pages continued to arrive from India, and although I still focused on my own life, I felt more and more responsible for Norman's recovery. He was being open with me about his illness and the emotional upheaval he was going through, and I wanted to tell him the important things in my life. His obvious devotion to me filled my long-standing need for someone to care for. My response was without hesitation.

1248 22 Avenue North
Seattle, Washington
November 1942

My dear, I am still here in Seattle. Have you had any of my letters answering your airgraphs? Are you getting good care? A friend of mine has told me that citrus fruits can help cure arthritis. Rationing has started here today but when I found a source of tiny cans of lemon juice and explained why I wanted many of them, they said I could have their whole stock, several dozen, without coupons. I will be allowed to send four at a time, once a month. I hope they reach you, though heaven knows how long it will take. With any luck your address will stay the same until they ship you home.

I eagerly await your next airgraph.

S/Ldr N.B. Silk
R.A.F Hospital
Calcutta, India
October 1942

Schlew! At last! One of those blue envelopes with your handwriting on it. You've only had two bits of mine! No matter, Sweeny, I know all my letters will find their way to you. My spirit is lightened by your understanding and warmth. Oh, my heart, what a joy it is to be in touch again. Sometimes I dream we walk and talk together upon the moors. Now I know it is a possibility. I'm going to be well, just you wait! It has been hell not knowing where you were, how you were and who was important in your life.

You have lost your father and because you loved him deeply it will have been a great sadness. I know that. Such a sudden growing up, taking your life in your hands, becoming professional. I want to know it all. There's so much catching up to do but writing will fill the hours whilst I await passage home. God, the transportation thing is hopeless. One man in my ward diagnosed with a brain tumour waited for four months before they put him on a ship to England to get an operation. How he stayed sane I can't imagine. I have been in five hospitals and everywhere I landed the specialists told me something different. The only thing they agree upon is that whatever I have, its incurable. They say exercise won't help me, but I know better. I don't listen to them any longer. Although I couldn't fire a bloody pistol if my life depended on it now because my fingers won't close tight enough, I can use them, as you can see, and I can lift a fairly heavy scrubbing mop above my head. It may not seem like much, but you should have seen me a month ago. I am actually putting on weight, six pounds since I hit bottom last January.

That's enough of my woes. I want to know all you can tell me about yourself, your work and your expectations with Ballet Theatre. Until this God-forsaken bloodletting is over, nothing is for sure, but I never stop building castles. It's the method I use to fight off almighty depression, and sometimes I just laugh. It's so damned ridiculous.

Here comes supper.

Beanachd Leibh,
Norman.

S/ Ldr N.B. Silk
R.A.F Hospital
Calcutta, India
November, 1942

Not only is Calcutta unbearably hot and filthy, but we seem to have been situated, wherever the service posts us, here or in Egypt, Palestine or South Africa, in the most depressingly squalid and hopeless bowels of cities. The last year since this arthritis got me has been utter hell, not only because of the pain, but the rapid setting-in of stiffness and loss of strength was infuriating. I could not fight my way out of depression that in itself almost killed me. The hospitals here are the bottom. Everything you ever heard about them is true. But even in my deepest discomfort I could find some relief thinking about family, imagining myself in the cool, high country walking free with old Morag on the hunt for rabbits. Mum has her now but I shall get her back! I am getting stronger each day and with any luck they'll send me home soon.

But do not be deceived, Sweeny. What my body and mind have been through cannot have failed to change me; in some ways for the better, I hope. Although I am much less civil, I am learning patience and a considerable amount of compassion. But I will never be able to live in a city or sit at a desk job. My body will need the out-of-doors and continuous exercise to get really fit again and remain that way. I hazard a guess that the forestry would train me and give me a job and I know of a croft at the head of Loch Etive that I think I can buy where life would be simple but could also be glorious. Wonderful for the upbringing of children, don't you think?

This wasn't exactly a proposal, yet surely a house and children came after marriage? Without a doubt I was getting very deeply into this relationship and I wanted it that way. But was this love? Sometimes the question of practicality rose above my romantic feelings and shed doubts about my ability to fill the role of Norman's wife should he not get all his strength back. A croft is a primitive abode, with few if any of the amenities one takes for granted these days, and Loch Etive was bound to be miles from nowhere. How I wished there was someone to talk to. Not Lily or Claude. Nor Miss Hart. I needed to know what was right to do: whether I should consider the difficulties of such a life as ours might turn out to be and get out while it was still possible—even though that would be letting Norman down—or continue to support him unselfishly. I thought of him as terribly brave and strong and wondered if I could be that strong—strong enough, that is, to stick it out if things got tough. But then, wasn't that the kind of challenge I wanted?

Did I feel real love for him? I thought I did. He loved me, anyway. I had been happy when I was with him. Was there anyone else I loved?

Not really. I would have married Pat if he'd wanted me, but that could have been a mistake. No other man I'd ever cared for could compare favourably with Norman. His enthusiasm and kindliness were worth more than Pat's or Claude's doctoral degrees. When he wrote of freedom of thought and mind from cynicism and the chains of excessive conventionalism I knew his thinking was progressive and that he could teach me a great deal about living. Was I afraid of the changes that must occur in my life if I decided to marry Norman? Sometimes.

Older people might have told me not to be so deeply concerned, told me that I was young and had lots of time. But I knew it was the present that mattered. It was what I said to Norman as he fought to get well that could help or hinder him. I was sure of that.

Whether or not I loved him then, I could feel that Norman had been extraordinarily patient. For months, for years, he had hoped for letters. Though I had been flippant and cutting when he had written to me after I came home from England, he hadn't retaliated. Now I understood that he'd simply waited for me to grow up, and I wanted to show him that I had. I needed his love.

Norman's determination to get well was bound to be a great help in his recovery. On the other hand, if he were to decide there was no hope for recovery, he'd likely refuse to marry me anyway. Having come to this conclusion, I decided to leave my worries to the higher power.

Gradually our letters became more intimate in the way we shared thoughts and expressed feelings, building higher and higher hopes and dreams of a future together. He told his early life's story and explored the dreams he had held dear since the time when we knew each other in London. These letters, though censored, were beautiful.

> I can see the hills grey-green and in the last of the sun
> the loch shines silver. We've been walking miles and miles,
> you and I. To swim now is most natural. We stand with the
> light upon our bodies on two high rocks that jut from out
> the shore, and when laughing from the sheer joy of it we
> dive, it is to meet under water and rise, face to face, body
> to body. So I dream.

And I replied, enjoying the feel of what I'd written,

> I hold the hand of a child whose braided hair is as dark
> as yours, but whose eyes are blue-violet. She dances over
> the heath weightless.

In one of his letters, Norman told me that after I had gone out of his life he had been tempted to become physically involved with a woman to whom he had been strongly attracted. "But," he said, "having promised myself that I would trace you one day when the war had been won, I didn't see her again." His admission only warmed and encouraged me.

All this was on my mind while I continued my own dance practice and, during the daily lessons, passed on my new skills as I acquired them. With the students I focused on clean line, perfection of detail and exactitude with music. Despite Constance Hart's gloom, student classes had new excitement, and, when she realized she was missing something, she could resist no longer. To my delight, she began turning up for my early morning practices. Though whenever possible she still avoided speaking to me, we maintained, nonetheless, a musical bond. Without my asking she played exactly what I needed for my work. Without exchanging words I was able to create several dances to exciting music that she dug out of her library and played for me. And, as the crucial day of my audition drew near, Constance encouraged me, came to the studio early and stayed on late at night.

On the particular Sunday morning in February when Alicia Markova had agreed to audition me for the American Ballet Theatre, Seattle was in the grip of a midwinter snowstorm. Before it was light and with much of the public transport system at a standstill, I set out to walk from Lily's house on 29th Avenue to Constance Hart's downtown studio. Because we had not been on speaking terms, I was surprised when at nine, booted and snow-covered, Miss Hart arrived to play for me. Without a word she sat at the piano and we began the warm-up, and for the hours prior to the audition, she played like an angel.

At ten, the appointed hour, Markova didn't appear. Nor was she there at ten-thirty or eleven. Still hopeful, Miss Hart and I continued to work till well after noon when Madam arrived. The world's best-loved ballerina had walked from her hotel in a foot of snow to see me audition.

"I have only ten minutes," she said. I thanked her for coming and introduced Miss Hart, who welcomed her, offered her a chair, then returned quickly to the piano. Still in her overshoes, Markova chose to sit with her back to the mirror, and I, in black tights and leotard, white ballet shoes and socks, with my hair tied firmly back under a white band, took my position at centre floor. Supported by Miss Hart's brilliant accompaniment I danced inspired for at least forty minutes—adagio and allegro, small batterie and grande leaps, changed to pointe shoes for pirouettes and classical variations and to bare feet for a robust Spanish gypsy piece—before sinking into my deepest curtsy.

In the silence, Markova asked, "Have you something more to show me?" I bowed. "Mr. Dolin must see you," she said.

Now this was a real compliment. Anton Dolin was probably Britain's most honoured *danseur*, a brilliant performer of character roles and the finest-ever supporting partner of prima ballerinas.

"You will have to catch him at the hotel before he leaves for the theatre. Just go up there at half past five and wait at the elevator. Introduce yourself. I'll tell him to expect you."

"I'll be there, Madam. I don't know how to thank you."

Miss Hart shook Markova's hand and went to open the door. Looking seriously at me, Miss Markova said, "Thank you, Anna," and swept out. I was suddenly tongue-tied. Having closed the door, Miss Hart turned and looked at me. For a long emotion-filled moment we didn't speak. Then we shared our first honest hug.

It took all my courage, but I spoke up when Anton Dolin stepped from the hotel elevator into the foyer. "Mr. Dolin," I said, "my name is Anna Verite. Miss Markova told me to intro..."

He looked my way. "So there you are," he interrupted, and kept walking toward the door.

"How do you do?" I managed to say as I walked beside him.

"Markova has told me about you," said he. "Says she wants me to see you dance."

"Oh, thank you, Mr. Dolin. Would you be so..."

He stopped and faced me. "Tell you what. Meet me backstage tomorrow evening at seven. I'll take a look, and you can tell me about yourself then. Don't be late."

"Thank you, Mr. Dolin, I'll be there on the dot," I said to his back as he walked away from me. I did it! I did it! I wanted to shout. Then I saw Markova coming toward me.

"Did he say he would see you, Anna?"

"Oh, yes, Miss Markova. Tomorrow before the performance, and thank you for this morning. Thank you for bothering on such a day."

"I enjoyed it," she replied warmly, "and aren't you lucky to have such a fine accompanist?"

"You are right," I agreed, feeling a fresh pang of guilt. "I am lucky indeed. I'll tell Miss Hart what you said."

"When you come to the theatre, ask the doorman to show you to my dressing room. Do give yourself time to warm up." Warmly dressed and still booted, Markova hurried to a waiting taxi.

Next evening, with the roads cleared, I found my way to the stage door of the civic auditorium and was shown to the dressing room where two of the world's greatest ballerinas, Alicia Markova and Alexandra Danilova, were preparing to perform. They were easy to talk to, and as I changed into practice clothes, Markova made suggestions about what Mr. Dolin would want to see. Then she showed me a quiet corner where I could warm up.

In the dim light behind the closed fire curtain, stagehands were still setting up the show, but one of them pushed aside lighting battens lying on the floor and pulled back hanging wires to make a space for me. Exactly on time Anton Dolin did indeed appear in full makeup as the terrifying Blue Beard –though still in his dressing gown–to conduct an exacting audition which went on to include a whole dance without music. But who needs music when it's all in your head? As my performance came to its dramatic end, I was surprised by applause. The shadowy wings had filled with company members.

Mr. Dolin asked, "Why haven't I seen you before?"

I told him I had lived within a stone's throw of his studio in Chelsea, but that in those days I knew I wasn't ready. He asked me a few more questions about my training; that I had studied with Nijinska seemed to be of most importance.

"Keep in touch," he said. "We'll be needing you."

From time to time during that spring, while I completed my second year of teaching in Seattle, both Markova and Dolin wrote to me from New York. They told me when rehearsals for the new season would begin at which time they hoped I would join them in Florida.

Though I still had difficulty seeing her side of the conflict we had locked ourselves into, from that time on Miss Hart broke her silence and every day showed me more of her friendly personality. In the end, despite the fact that I was leaving her, she generously supported and encouraged my dream.

After my audition, the CAS invited me to join as lead dancer and assistant choreographer.

CHAPTER 5

Private Sweeny, CWAC

I n June, with the term ended and the student concert over, I said my good-byes to Constance Hart, her school of dance, to Lily, Claude and all their family and to Seattle. I took a bus to Vancouver for a holiday with Mum while waiting for news from the Ballet Theatre.

Mum's door had hardly closed when there was a telephone call from Uncle Dick. I had been slow to recognize it, but now saw that ever since Dad's death, Uncle Dick had been taking special care of me. And what he had to say in his phone call decidedly stirred my interest. Would I like to meet his friend Major Victor George who was in command of a big military entertainment company presently playing in Vancouver?

Uncle Dick explained that it was his responsibility, even though he was a civilian, to administer the box-office receipts from the Vancouver performances of this show in aid of B.C. Armed Services Canteens. He said that the show's cast had been recruited from all across the country and that everywhere they played, the company held talent auditions. "I rattled off a few of your dance qualifications," said my uncle. "Must have done a good sales job because Vic suggested you should accompany him to a performance."

My head swam. I kept saying, "Thank you, thank you so much."

"I have given Major George your mother's telephone number. You can expect his call momentarily."

And that was how, the following night, I came to be escorted on the arm of the Commanding Officer of the Canadian Army Show to the best seat in Vancouver's old Strand Theatre.

From the overture on, the show was vibrant. It was big and extravagant, fast and funny, but it was touching and beautiful too. I wasn't able find a thing to criticise.

Of course I would audition for CAS! I was enchanted and enormously impressed but, trying to appear nonchalant, I hesitated just a moment before thanking Major George and promising to think about his offer of an audition. I had to admit that the idea was tempting. Dancing in the Army Show would be so easy and such fun. Not only that, I'd be back with Canadians, where I belonged.

Two days later, on June 29, 1943, with Corporal Denny Vaughan at a piano on the empty bandstand, I danced for a handful of Army Show top brass on the slippery floor of the ballroom in the Old Hotel Vancouver on Granville opposite the Birks building. Seated in a stiff little row on the dance floor just in front of the stage, the group included Captain Romney Brent, who was the show's production officer, Lieutenant Lisa Lineaweaver, the show's lead dancer as well as officer in charge of CWACs, and Captain Rai Purdy, in charge of radio broadcasting.

Feeling quite relaxed and sure of myself and especially pleased that Corporal Vaughan found no difficulty in playing my music, I recalled Mr. Dolin's enthusiasm during my audition in Seattle and asked the corporal to play that same fiery gypsy number. Then casually, without waiting to be asked, I continued with a string of fast turns. Flashing a smile in their direction, I sauntered to centre floor for my next demonstration, but Lieutenant Lineaweaver waved her hand in a "that's all" gesture. The audition was over.

For a few minutes the officers huddled near the stage whispering, while I stood in the middle of that empty ballroom surrounded by the glow of my own self-importance. Suddenly another light came on; they might not want me. Had I been too flippant? Might I, after all, have to return to the ugliness of theatre life as I had so far experienced it? I felt myself shrink. I closed my eyes and saw Ballet Theatre—not the thrill of performance with them, but the long battle I knew I'd have to fight, using the tools those girls in Hollywood had shown me, to get where I wanted to go. I'd have to struggle through inevitably cruel politics to rise from corps de ballet–I could never settle for that–to reach any degree of stardom. In contrast, with the army as my employer, I would have few, if any, decisions to make and there would be no games to play.

After what seemed like forever, Captain Brent called me over. "Thank you for coming," he said in his polite English voice. "Should I call you Miss Verite or Miss Sweeny?

Not sure who I was at that moment, I answered, "Either, I suppose."

Then he asked in a voice that sounded like thanks-but-no-thanks, "Would you consider joining the company? And if so, becoming a soldier?" My heart had pounded alive again by the time he added, "How soon could you enlist should you choose to serve?"

I was right back on my cloud.

At that moment, Lieutenant Lineaweaver added a most juicy enticement. "It is rumoured," she said, "that the show may soon be ordered overseas to a base in England."

Safe in my renewed confidence I said, "I'm sorry to be difficult, but I am waiting for another contract. I can't answer you immediately."

Next day, at Uncle's Dick's suggestion, we concocted a telegram to American Ballet Theatre to hurry their decision. By return telegram came my most-wished-for-positive-answer: "Anna Verite should join company Florida August fifteen." The moment was euphoric. I was good enough! They did want me! And soon! My confidence soared. But along with it came a whiff of anxiety, something to do with dancing for the rest of my life, to do with my disenchantment with Hollywood. Though I had the contract I'd worked so hard for, and I knew I was capable, I astonished myself by deciding–with hardly a gulp–to give up my stage name and postpone my ballet career to join the Canadian Army Show. I asked Uncle Dick to tell Major George I was ready to become a soldier. "Glad to have you," was his response. He also offered me both the position of lead dancer for the company and assistant to the choreographer. Now I felt sure I had made the right choice.

My acceptance probably pleased the traditional members of my family, some of whom saw my theatrical career as embarrassing. Family members and everyone else I spoke to appeared to be enthusiastic about my change of plans. "After all," they said, "the war's in its fourth year. It can't last much longer."

The recruiting office was in the same Old Hotel Vancouver where I had auditioned in the grand ballroom. I forget the exact process I went through to become a soldier, except that it happened rapidly. There were forms to fill in, IQ tests to write, medical tests and inoculations for a raft of possible sicknesses. Then I was issued a number (W 110-975, Sweeny V.), was sworn in and ordered to report to CWAC Headquarters barracks on Vancouver's Little Mountain, where a platoon sergeant gave me a summer uniform. She also supplied a Canada badge that was to be sewn just below the shoulder of my tunic, and a black maple leaf on a yellow circle to go just below it. I received a weekend pass and went back to Mum's apartment where she gave me a handful of airgrams that had been forwarded to Vancouver by Lily Johnson. That night I wrote Norman to tell him my new plan, hinting that the unit might be sent overseas. By that Sunday afternoon in mid-July 1943, dressed in my crisp uniform, I thought of myself with a new kind of pride as Private Sweeny. So anxious was I to begin my new life, I said good-bye to Mum hours earlier than necessary and returned to Little Mountain for indoctrination.

Two weeks after signing up, I was off to basic training with a platoon of CWACs. Having sat up all the way from Vancouver, we detrained at Vermilion, Alberta at 0200 hours. The temperature was below freezing when we stumbled onto the platform. Shivering in our summer uniforms, we were marched to trucks which delivered our kit bags to barracks and us to quartermaster stores. In single file we marched past a counter with our arms stretched forward to be loaded with blankets by one private, a pillow and towel by another.

"Chin up!" snapped the sergeant at the end of the line, stuffing a package of sanitary napkins firmly under each girl's chin. Then out we went into the moonlight, carrying our new possessions along icy wooden pathways to the main building. There we were told we could dump our kit in our quarters and come to the mess hall for a bowl of soup. Dawn broke as we finally fell onto hard bunks.

For me there were many familiar aspects to military life because my family background was military. In uniform, therefore, I became W 110-975 Private Sweeny V with a certain pleasure and didn't have to think too much about protocol. I already knew that I must call other service people by the surname used for roll-call and pay-parade. Although I understood that sir or ma'am sufficed for addressing an officer, as a private I had to learn to jump when a sergeant barked. I would learn how to salute an officer, obey standing orders and grasp army law, properly launder a shirt, and shine my brass buttons, Athena collar-pins and cap-badge without getting Brasso on my uniform. I learned how to peel potatoes with a machine, scrub latrines and sing marching songs. One exercise my platoon would perfect—that of polishing our platoon corridor by dragging the largest CWAC from one end to the other by her feet, her ass upon a couple of issue sanitary napkins—would make a joke of the whole nitpicking, platoon quarters inspection.

But it wouldn't all be fun. Many of my platoon would have blistered feet, and inoculations would cause some women considerable discomfort. I learned how to march, not an easy thing for a dancer. With stiff arms, my fingers in a fist, thumbs pressed hard against the first joints of my first fingers, I had to learn to swing my arms without moving my head or shoulders, striding ahead heel-first with my toes pointing straight forward and up.

But I took to route marching with gusto. Although my legs were a bit short, my naturally long stride was perfect for marching in a column. I have always stood tall anyway, the only changes I had to make were to lessen the swing of my hips and hold my shoulders straight to the front while my arms alternated. And since I soon showed them I knew my left foot from my right, they made me marker, the pivotal position for forming platoon and for changing direction in column of route. I had a good loud bark, too, from years of shouting over music to teach dancers and also from my natural enthusiasm, so I became an acting drill-sergeant.

"Paraaaade......a.....tennnn.....*wait for it!*...shun, one two. Paraaaade ...by the left, qui...ick....march! LEFT right, LEFT right...By the left, left wheel, LEFT right LEFT right, LEFT right, LEFT right...Paraaaaaade...Halt! One two."

The army took it easy on us at first, only marched us a mile and back with a five-minute stand easy between. New shoes caused lots of blisters and some of our platoon found even a two-mile hike pretty tiring, but my feet were already tough from dancing, so four miles and even six miles were no sweat.

Very few excuses could get a person off a route march, but I welcomed marches whatever the weather. They were considered good for the constitution generally, excellent for hangovers, the best thing for shedding a cold and a necessity for toughening the feet. Marches were great for the lungs, and for singing and shouting "left, left, he had a good job but he left," and they were the absolute answer to arms sore from injections. "The exercise will spread the serum around and lessen the pain," explained Sergeant Roberts.

For me, parades were fun too, but there were hazards involved in parading; heat and cold were the most quickly obvious. My earliest days of learning to stand on parade were in August and September when daytime temperatures at Vermilion could, and often did, reach 90 degrees Fahrenheit, although, as temperatures nightly dropped to freezing, by evening we were shivering in our summer uniforms. Daily parades kept us looking smart and instilled the drill in our minds. However, inspection of a full company, especially with visiting dignitaries, could take a long time when one had to stand absolutely still, feet together, chest up, chin in and eyes front. Day after day, CWACs fainted and fell out of line, usually suffering from the effects of inoculations, but sometimes from holding their breath or being too tense. Sometimes just the heat would do it. I reacted to booster shots by fainting on that scorched parade square. We learned the routine: the two closest to the fainter would "clear the victim's tongue and put the cap over the head." An NCO would "bring a pencil to put between the teeth." No one else moved to help. The sun shone, the wind blew or the rain rained, but the parade continued. When the CWAC came to, she'd be walked off the square.

Daily, the physical demands grew tougher and our brains were pushed to absorb more information. At night we were exhausted when we crawled under our grey army blankets.

Of course, I hadn't heard from Norman since leaving Vancouver and I'd had no time to write to him. However, within a few weeks I received a letter from Anton Dolin, sent to me in care of Uncle Dick's office, in which he congratulated me for choosing to serve my country. His letter also encouraged me to believe I would have a successful ballet career as soon as the war ended. I didn't cry until much later. For now, anyway, I had to trust that Markova and Dolin would still want me later—much later, as it turned out, than anyone could have predicted.

Near the end of basic training, as we grew strong and our confidence returned, we began to laugh again. By the fifth Monday our shoulders had relaxed, as well as the creases between our eyebrows, just in time for the announcement that gas drill would take place on Thursday. We'd heard about it the very first day but I'd been too busy to worry in advance, so it came as a remembered blow.

When Thursday dawned, I awoke with depression and a stabbing fear. Shivering, I rolled off my bunk without my usual "good morning!" and went off to shower. We were all scared. No one mentioned the order of the day. Parade and breakfast were over, and we were writing a test on military law when an announcement on the tannoy reminded us to parade in full dress at 1100 hours. Full dress included tin hat and respirator. I felt a chill around my neck and down my back and drew in a deep breath, holding it momentarily before letting it go, resigned to the inevitable. I took some comfort knowing I wouldn't be alone, also that it must be safe since everyone before me had carried on without lasting effect.

Nervous chatter erupted now and then from the otherwise solemn platoon of young women who stood easy at the edge of a parade square awaiting orders from the drill sergeant. "Platoon!" We shut up, clasped our hands loosely behind our backs and listened. "Platoon, atten...shun!" We brought our thumbs to our sides as our left feet struck the ground hard beside the right. "Stand at...ease!" Left feet slapped wide again as the hands went back. "Stand easy. Prepare to don respirators!"

We stuffed our caps into our haversacks, and unbuckled the straps on our respirators.

"You will enter the chamber single file and obey orders," snapped Sergeant Roberts. "Don respirators!" She gave us no more than thirty seconds to extract the masks from their cases, adjust them over our faces and snap on our tin hats while she did the same. "Platoon..." It sounded peculiar from inside her mask. Our hands went behind our backs. "Platoon, at-ten...shun. Platoon...le-eft turn." She marched to take her place at the head of the three files. For the first time I felt real fear. "By the left...qui-ick march!" I might as well have been headed for execution.

We followed Sergeant Roberts off the parade square, wheeling left up a road past Administration to where a square, windowless army hut stood at the outskirts of camp with its door open. Here our platoon halted in a shambles because we hadn't heard the muffled order. Listening more carefully now, we right-faced and stood at ease, then stood easy. Sticking her fingers between her mask and her chin, Sergeant Roberts shouted at us to check the fit of the face piece, demonstrating the tab that could be adjusted. When everyone had stopped fussing, she called us to attention, shouted that the three files should proceed singly from the left, and went ahead to stand outside the door. As marker, I obediently led the way into a brightly lit room. Inside, another instructor formed us into four rows. When everyone, including Sergeant Roberts, had come in, the door was closed. Very soon a yellowish mist began to appear from a vent in the ceiling. As the gas thickened, we were instructed to walk about, and it swirled around us like fog as we followed one another in a circle moving faster and faster. Although tempted to hold my breath, I eventually had to breathe and found that I could, quite easily, through the filter. In a minute or so, the sergeants directed us into four lines across the room where we halted and, for several minutes, performed exercises touching our toes and swinging our arms. Then we were instructed to remove our face masks and hold them in our left hands. "Go on, do it *now!*" they said together. They didn't take theirs off!

There was no way out. The masks came off and the circle began again. The air felt thick and smelt horrible. "Move! Move on! Keep moving and keep breathing. You must breathe." And with that, the sergeants upped the pace to a jog and circled us twice around the room before opening the door and leading us out. Right away Sergeant Roberts ordered the platoon to form and stood us easy. She instructed us to replace our masks. Under no circumstances, she told us, should we take them off for the next fifteen minutes, even if we felt sick. Even if we vomited.

The best thing to do, she said, was to keep walking about and breathing as normally as possible. Already I felt nauseous. The temptation to remove the mask grew greater by the second. As soon as she ordered, "Break off," we dispersed onto a grassy patch and began walking. I wanted to lie down and cry but instead I began to cough. Hold on! Hold on, I said to myself. You don't have to be sick. Just keep breathing steadily, but I couldn't. My eyes were weeping, my nose felt full, the cough was coming from deep inside and I was retching, heaving, gagging and up it came. A mouthful of slime shot into the face piece. I knew it partially blocked the air vent because I had to gasp for air but fortunately the intake was a fairly wide tube. I continued to heave, but only saliva flowed. It was just luck that I hadn't eaten much breakfast. The heaving eventually subsided and I looked about to see how the rest had fared. One or two had already removed their masks, but it didn't feel much like fifteen minutes. I began to feel terribly sad, would have loved to lie down right where I was, but somehow kept walking until I got to where one of the sergeants stood watching.

"You all right?" she asked.

"Yes," I mumbled. "When can I take this thing off?"

"Any time you want now," she said. "Not much fun, is it? Did you muck up your respirator?" I nodded. "Better clean it up." I pulled doggedly at the beastly thing. "Don't go to lunch parade. You'll likely feel pretty depressed for a while. Take it easy for the afternoon. You'll be okay by dinner time!"

All I can remember, after that, is sitting very forlornly on a bench with some other CWACs thinking, so this is what depression feels like!

The idea of this exercise, of course, was to instill into us the understanding that a bit of mustard gas could make a person sick, but a lot of it could kill. One must keep going and keep trying to breathe inside one's respirator, no matter what!

By mid September, I had passed all my tests and was shipped home to CWAC Western HQ to await posting. A few days of leave in Mum's minuscule apartment gave us time for some long overdue heart-to-heart talks.

Although we didn't actually discuss his death, Mum shared with me in a way she never had before, tender things about Dad from before their marriage and expressed her gratitude that he had been there for her when Gerry had been killed. We discussed the present, gruelling life of my elder brother, Sedley, with the Royal Engineers, and we finally spoke of my brother Malcolm's disappearance at sea in 1936. Mum brought me up to date on Moira's accomplishments; having become a WRCN at eighteen, she was already a decoder. Roger, my third brother, although too young to enlist, would soon go to Royal Roads and the Navy. But more than anything, Mum talked affectionately about Dad, and she gave me a poem he had sent to her from away up north when forced to accept any job he could find during the 1920s. I was less than two years old at that time. He must have been terribly lonely for all of us when he wrote:

To love his own is given unto man 'small time'
For if he dreams, their happy smiles depart
And if he strives his thoughts must fly away
For most, if not for all his wakeful day.

And so it is with me–whose children lived

So full of sunshine, crammed with life

When I beheld them last–I may not see again

till childhood's past.

He went on to describe how he yearned:

To spend his time just teaching you to live

To romp with you and utterly enjoy

Each moment of your lives...

He said that this would be joy unbounded, and he signed it, S.F.C.S., Anyox, Feb. 4, 1924.

I had difficulty holding back tears.

Mum told me that though she had loved and admired Dad, she had continued to hold an important place in her heart for Gerry. As she explained how torn she had been when Dad asked her to marry him, I felt sympathy for her. But I also understood something of Dad's loneliness. Oddly, this seemed to be the right time to talk about my grief over Pat's departure from my life.

Mum had held onto several of Norman's letters for me. From one I learned that he'd soon have his passage home to England. I told her how supportive of him I felt after his illness and let her know that he was my closest friend. I didn't tell her that Norman had hinted at marriage, but I did say I dearly hoped to be sent overseas. I needed to know him again in person because so much had happened to us both since I'd left England.

Then, in late September 1943 I entrained for Toronto where I marched myself into an incredible adventure which would grow me up considerably.

Captain Rai Purdy with Acting Lieutenant Lisa Lineaweaver, OC CWACs.

CHAPTER 6

Shuster and Wayne and the Army Show Command Performance

About a year before I joined up, the first fully-fledged Canadian Army Show production had been choreographed in Toronto by Aida Broadbent, a very successful Canadian who worked out of Hollywood. That was all I knew about her then. No wonder I had been impressed, had literally gasped at the grandeur of her work, when I saw the show in Vancouver the following summer; apart from the lavish production she had created for the Festival of Roses in the California Rose Bowl, Aida was already the most sought-after choreographer in Hollywood. There were many stars who wouldn't make a movie without Aida Broadbent. Her work kept her on the road worldwide.

But for all the importance of her name then, in 1942 it must have delighted Aida to be brought home by the Canadian government to choreograph a first-class variety show. She'd have the best possible technical facilities, luscious live music and a stable of outstanding talent to work with.

The fast-rising comedy team of Frank Shuster and Johnnie Wayne had been offered top billing and would be supported by comediennes Mildred Morey and Connie Vernon, both now CWAC sergeants. Backed by both male and female choirs, two very popular solo voices already well known on radio–"Golden-Voiced Jimmy Shields" and opera tenor Roger Doucet could be counted on to pluck the heartstrings. Ballad singer Raymonde Maranda and mellow-toned Mary Moynahan were also seasoned performers.

A whole platoon of CWAC dancers, all of them young, talented and well trained, awaited Aida. An adept group of male dancers could also double as actors and singers. An adagio ballroom team and numerous variety acts had been hired. The cast was nearly complete. Plans were in place for elaborate sets and extravagant costumes, and music, with an extra-large string section, was to be under the batons of Captains Geoffrey Waddington and the brilliant composer/arranger Captain Robert Farnon. Indeed, *live* music, nowadays so often replaced by recordings in theatres, would take charge of the Army Show from the overture onward. Some staff members were from the Toronto Symphony, others, Canada's top recording musicians. Nothing but the best for Bob Farnon. Already well-known, he was heading for a fabulous career making music for films. There would also be a sizzling jazz band. Under the guidance of highly respected theatre producer Jack Arthur, Aida Broadbent would have much to do with shaping the show around its illustrious cast. She returned to the USA in the late spring of 1943, by which time the production was ready for its first cross-country tour. In July, when the show played Vancouver, it literally enchanted me, its dazzling choreographic effects–Aida's trademark– may have been one of the catalysts for my becoming a soldier.

Back in Toronto, following that jubilant national tour, the cast had been given two weeks leave. Then, while I was taking my basic training in Alberta, they refreshed their military skills at a camp in Ontario. Upon their return to the company, featured performers and some more senior personnel had been given promotions to higher ranks which carried authority and responsibility and raised their pay–slightly.

When I finally reached Toronto, someone collected me at Union Station and delivered me to CWAC headquarters at Queen's Park. It was dinner time in the mess-hall when I met the CAS CWACs for the first time. A cheery lot, they were expecting me and showed me around the dark old mansion. The women slept on metal cots, four or five to a bedroom, with duffle bags and haversacks stuffed underneath. This was the kind of accommodation I had expected, but in the bathrooms, the trickles of silverfish crawling up from the drain pipes threatened to take the starch out of me.

The first morning, it was all I could do to swallow anything at breakfast, where the menu was runny oatmeal, square eggs (dehydrated and boxed army-style), toast and bacon. The bacon, having been set out on trays and placed in the oven the night before, appeared on the breakfast table with a generous sprinkling of baked cockroaches. So far, I had been issued neither battle-dress (rough khaki pants and monkey jacket) like the other CWACs, nor greatcoat. Accustomed to Vancouver's gentle climate, I shivered from the sharp change in temperature. Still wearing my tight uniform skirt and tunic to go to CAS headquarters at the Victoria Theatre, I found it awkward and embarrassing to be boosted aboard a troop carrier with an MT driver's hand on my backside.

When I actually arrived at the theatre, I discovered that the company had been in rehearsal for several weeks. The cast and production team, with a fabulous season behind them and filled with understandable optimism, were preparing a new version of "It's the Army Show" to take on tour again come spring. To give a fresh look to the chorus and production numbers, a civilian, Felicia Sorrel, had been hired from New York as the temporary dance director. Although there was new talent in the company, I learned that the original comedy material and sketches were only being revamped and the opening and closing as well as several of Aida's production numbers were to remain intact. Although my official title was lead dancer and assistant choreographer, the new rehearsal schedule was already in place without any input from me. I wasn't assigned any particular job but was told to attend production meetings and observe activities in wardrobe, the scene shop, back stage, dressing rooms and administrative offices.

I was acutely disappointed not to be immediately given work with some authority. Still, the pressure of adjusting to new barracks and the Victoria Theatre as well as learning to find my way about as a new member of an established company kept me occupied and helped me not to feel altogether superfluous. And I could look forward to taking my proper place when Miss Sorrell departed.

Felicia Sorrell was short and plump. She usually dressed in black trousers and tops and wore her mass of black, curly hair in a snood with–I counted them–seven slides and clips of various colours to hold her unruly mop together. Her scarlet lipstick emphasized the darkness of her Latin complexion and matched the polish on her long finger-nails. Felicia smoked almost continuously and her sultry voice suggested she had been at it a long time. Her hips moved as though they were motorized, which wasn't surprising since she claimed to be the Black Bottom Queen of New York. Although this dance was popular at the time, I felt Felicia was out of her element here, Black Bottom not being the style of the Army Show. However, since I expected to assist her, I tried not to be negative.

Following my audition in Vancouver, I hadn't had a single opportunity to practise and had hardly given my own technique a thought. The thrill of having been accepted had been enough to maintain my enthusiasm. Now I wanted to learn the show as fast as possible and prove my worth as an instructor.

Within a few weeks I became a lance corporal. I had to ask where to sew my first stripe and had hardly become used to seeing it on my sleeve when a memo came to me from the orderly room: "Corporal Sweeny contact Colonel Sweeny at #12 Depot, New Toronto." This reminded me that Uncle Bims, my father's elder brother, was also back in uniform in the Veterans' Guard, though I hadn't known he was stationed near Toronto.

"Good Lord, child," he shouted at me on his arrival outside the theatre–all my family seemed to shout–"Where have you been all my life?"

It was a typical remark. Tall and terribly handsome in his tartan trews with a Seaforth Glengarry, he strode to where I waited with my military pass in my hand. Thank heaven, before I could salute he hugged me. Then, taking me by the arm, he held open the door of a taxi and like the charmer he was, bowed me in.

"Thought a taxi'd be more fun than a staff car," my uncle said, beaming. I had always adored him. "Where would you like to go, kid? See a show or something?" We decided on vaudeville. He directed the driver and we sat back to chat.

I learned that he was in charge of a prisoner-of-war camp just outside the city. In his offhand way, so unlike my father, he recounted amusing stories about the German prisoners in the camp, how they occasionally tried to escape, how clever they were with their hands, making works of art with next to nothing, how friendly they were and how grateful they were to be out of the fighting. Although I wanted to, we didn't talk about Dad's death.

What we saw that night was really a girlie show and a very bad one at that. We laughed a lot and afterwards he took me to his mess. I knew this was out of bounds for a lance corporal, but he was my uncle and I concluded he must know what he was doing. Still, worried about what the other officers might think, I hesitated at the mess door.

"Come along," he said, crooking an elbow for me to tuck my arm into. "Let me introduce you to my friends. Gentlemen!" he bellowed as we entered the large, wood-panelled room, "may I present my girlfriend, Verity." Although I felt my face flush, they were indeed his friends, and they made me very welcome. Uncle Bims was, I suppose, in his mid-fifties at that time and I just twenty-one. What a lark! I didn't see him again until the war was over.

Although I lived with other CWACs, slept in dorms, ate in other ranks' (ORs') mess halls, travelled in trucks, sang marching songs and worked with dancers, singers, musicians, actors and stagehands, I never felt that I really belonged with the members of the cast. They were up on all that was current, knew the slang, who was who in movies and on records and had their favourites. So I listened, copied and mimicked, hoping that soon I could make up for being different by doing what I had come to do, dance.

Because of the breadth of my training, I understood almost any style of dance: Spanish, modern, tap, most ethnic styles from Europe and the Middle East. And when I did officially become Felicia's assistant, I did my best to interpret her Brooklyn wiggles and gyrations and to translate them into recognizable language for the chorus dancers. But the girls were, in fact, more in tune with Felicia than I was; quite quickly they achieved the sultry Latin look she was after for the new "Viva El Furlough" production number. Surprisingly, I too adapted to her style satisfactorily, and when the piece was nearly complete, Felicia gave me the solo in it. Not having danced for over four months, I was glad to find my own technique was still intact.

In the theatre, I lived in rehearsal clothes, and though a mere lance corporal, I found it easy enough to converse with the production officers—Captains Farnon, Brent, and Purdy. They invited me to attend after-hours production meetings that often went on long after the other CWACs in the show had returned to barracks. Usually one of the officers—who all had their own staff cars—drove me back to Queen's Park.

Out of the haze of my recollections there comes a picture of some of those meetings having taken place in one of the officers' sleeping quarters. Lieutenant Lineaweaver was there, though Felicia was not. Scenery and props-manager Sergeant Jim Hozack, a big fellow whose confidence made me feel he knew his job, and Captains Brent and Purdy were there. In fact, the meetings may have been in Captain Purdy's quarters in one of Toronto's elderly hotels. Anyway, in the generous atmosphere of rye and Coke, I was accepted as a member of the CAS production crew.

By the time they joined the army in 1942, Frank Shuster and Johnny Wayne—known then as Franky and Johnny—were a team of experienced comedians. A couple of hucksters by nature, they both stood short and tough on widely placed, self-assured feet. Their features were quickly recognizable. Frank played the straight man and Johnny was the nut who made great use of his bristling eyebrows and took most of the laughs. They had graduated from the University of Toronto one year apart, both with English degrees, and they both happened to thrive on Shakespeare, not only for the usual reasons—his use of language, rhythm and pace—but because the bard's plots and characters leaned so willingly into modern farce-comedy. Re-writing bits of these plays and creating a steady stream of new material, Franky and Johnny had been in their element at Hart House Theatre where they wowed the mainly student audiences.

I had seen Shuster and Wayne for the first time when the Army Show played in Vancouver. To the delight of every student of English and history buff, they had turned their knowledge and love of language upside-down. Their material showed no respect for authority. Lampooning without mercy, they were perfectly at ease making the high-ranking army officials from Ottawa the butt of their jokes. Like everyone else I had laughed till the tears ran. They could even dance, or at least jitterbug.

Because I'd lived outside Canada, this duo was completely new to me, and even after I became a soldier and joined the company in Toronto, I still didn't understand that theirs were already "big names."

Although the rest of the cast treated Shuster and Wayne with great respect and laughed at everything they said, it seemed to me their off-stage behaviour was uncomfortably loud and pushy. When I learned that they had written all their own material as well as sketches and lyrics for the body of the show, I wasn't so surprised at their self-satisfaction. In some respects, Shuster and Wayne *were* the show. Because their writing was extremely clever and they rehearsed their material tirelessly, they were thoroughly successful with their boisterous comedy routines. I had to admit that their dialogue, though suggestive, was clean and their humour never hurt. But offstage Wayne, especially, spoke in a voice that demanded attention. For all their success onstage, the applause never seemed to be enough.

Although they regularly poked fun at army regulations, they were proud to be Canadians. Following many successful appearances on the Ed Sullivan Show, billed by then as Wayne and Shuster, Canada's top comedy team, they turned down further American offers, returned to Canadian radio and, when the CBC-TV gave them their own weekly show, became household names across this country. Throughout their careers, Wayne and Shuster continued to maintain their Canadian integrity, never stooping to the competitive level of brutality typical of the then-rising breed of comics.

Indeed, I had accepted as particularly special the homespun, typically Canadian kind of honesty which had pervaded the first CAS show I saw. The performers had been different and interesting enough that there was no need for vulgarity. It wasn't all razzamatazz. Some of the vocals were deliberately touching, even sobering, as was the dramatic finale. Keeping in mind the soldiers' feelings for their wives and sweethearts, the girls had been presented with respect.

To me, Private Mary Moynihan was the perfect symbol of the girl left behind. Statuesque, she carried herself with grace, wore a gentle expression and radiated warmth with her mezzo-soprano voice. Mary wore a white, floor-length gown of rich material on the bosom of which shone a simple gold cross. It was said that she received many fan letters from servicemen.

Since our meeting in Vancouver, Lieutenant Lisa Lineaweaver, the CWAC administrative officer, had been promoted to captain and had retired as a performer. As lead dancer, I now replaced her and inherited her dance partner, Corporal Everett Staples. I had qualms that this might not be a happy change for him, not only because he and Lisa had enjoyed a most successful partnership—their style was elegant, smooth and sensuous, ballroom at its best—but also because his and my styles were somewhat mismatched. Ev's work was modern and full of sensuality while mine was classical and conservative. I was concerned about being a disappointment to him. However, his patience worked miracles. Ev taught me to walk in various sexy ways and explained that it was necessary that I "melt" my body to move smoothly with his. After only a few rehearsals we danced really well together.

Ev and I chose David Rose's "Holiday for Strings," popular at the time, for our first show number. It was ideal for the Farnon orchestra as well as the perfect medium for a mixture of modern and classical dance. Since Felicia used the stage most of the day to rehearse the

South American production, we had to make time to create "Holiday" when I wasn't in a production meeting or during the other dancers' lunch-hour. The two of us agreed that the opening phrases of "Holiday for Strings" sounded like fast feet running down hill, then up over hillocks–like flying across fields–leaping puddles–like spinning and laughing. And then the refrain, like a river in flood, seemed to pull us with it in great sweeping moves that paused and then, changing direction, rushed on again in curves that lifted and swirled us. The dance that evolved was almost balletic, really technical in the fast parts, then it simply flowed through the melodic bridges. It was a test for us to be fast and precise again when the joyous theme returned.

As well as being a most talented dancer, Ev was also costume designer for the whole show. Together we chose cream-coloured silk jersey for the dress he created for me in wardrobe. Since I would be wearing only briefs under it, he made no apology for building the dress on the nearly-bare me. To a wide elastic waistband tightly encircling my ribs, he attached two small pleated sections of the fabric to barely cover my minute dancer's breasts. These pleated strips passed over my shoulders and were anchored firmly at the back of the waistband. He cut the full circular skirt to flare gently from the same high waistline and to fall to within a breath of the floor. It was intended that it should sometimes wrap close about me then, unwinding, float in wide arcs and circles to show my legs and the fine gold sandals that would criss-cross my feet. Ev said he'd give me long aqua-coloured gloves and would finish the picture with a whisk of aqua net to circle my face from under my chin to the top of my head where he would tie it, with a generous flourish, into an upsweep of my red curls.

I pictured myself starring in the very show that had captured me. But I had little time for dreaming. Rehearsals in the Victoria Theatre kept me occupied, leaving barely time for Ev and me to polish our duo.

In November, the theatre lights were on around the clock. While dancers rehearsed on the stage, individual sketches were dreamed up, written and came to life upstairs and downstairs, in the green room, the canteen, offices, corridors and the lobby. I saw and heard very little of the comedy, the meat of the show, until it came on stage to be melded into full-blown scenes and acts, some already in costume.

In a building next to the theatre, filling the air with a rich cacophony, alternate conductors Waddington and Farnon fitted Farnon's new arrangements into the original score. They rehearsed the overture and fanfares, entrances and exits, backgrounds and features, solo voices and vocal chorus numbers as well as the major production numbers. All of the solo artists were preparing new material, but some would be repeating their most popular numbers.

Two weeks before the show's scheduled reopening, my rank was raised to full corporal. That day a memo in daily orders reported a request from CMHQ Ottawa for a command performance, no less! Working flat-out already, we redoubled our efforts toward an even earlier opening night–November 19. As the date approached, the company rehearsed longer and longer hours, a new rumour flew about imminent overseas marching orders for the whole company, and Ev and Lisa decided they would dance "Bolero" once more for the command performance.

Costume fittings happened in the wings whenever a dancer could be spared. Without interrupting rehearsals, the lighting director tested his lighting plot, and public-address systems were checked by the sound specialists. Performers put more and more energy into their work. Stagehands painted new reference markings on the stage floor, ready for Wednesday's "rough" dress rehearsal, and on that night the excitement and energy were contagious.

On Thursday night, with a large invited audience to see the "full dress," we heard the overture. A chill ran up my spine. Over the applause, Farnon's fanfare introduced the impressive opening production, and as one act followed another, Bob's rich arrangements supported them with imaginative backgrounds and flourishes for exits. Having the orchestra in the pit was magically pulling the show together. Although neither of our costumes was ready, when our cue came, Ev and I whirled blissfully through "Holiday" without a hitch, in practise dress.

There wasn't a moment's pause between acts and production numbers, which were never tedious or overly long. Running gags, black-out sketches, false starts, drum rolls and musical stings packed everything in tightly to keep the audience breathless, wanting more. Even on this first full run-through, there was hardly a moment's pause in the running order.

Suddenly there it was! Opening night. Extra special for me because it was my debut with the company. Lisa Lineaweaver, Sergeants Connie Vernon, Audrey Shields, Mildred Morey and Linda Tuero shared the female stars' dressing room. My rank of corporal gave me no extra privileges. Shoulder to bare shoulder with other CWACs before our mirrors in the chorus dressing room at the old Victoria Theatre, like the rest of them I wore my hair pulled back under a kerchief for makeup. To be sure the pancake didn't miss a single spot, we had our government issue dressing gowns tied by the sleeves around our waists, and alternately helped each other by daubing pancake on hard-to-reach, middle-of-the-back places, and checking each other's ears and necks.

The opening and closing numbers were strictly military, and the girls who were preparing to perform them kept complete uniforms with fresh shirts and pressed ties hanging on racks in the dressing room. Because of sweat and makeup smudges, the cleaning bill for these uniforms must have been enormous. The brass on them fairly gleamed because it was lacquered—an absolute no-no for regular uniforms which must show freshly shined brass every day or a CWAC could expect extra "fatigues."

The buzz of conversation in our dressing room was low so that above our heads we could hear the stagehands setting up for the show. Surprisingly, we didn't talk much but there was the odd outburst. "Gees! Why can't I make this eyelash stick?" Getting ready gave us far too much to do to be really nervous. But now and then I swallowed and took a deep breath, feeling my heart thud heavily when the enormity of this performance hit me straight on. I wasn't afraid of the South American production in the second half of the program. It was "Holiday for Strings" that concerned me. Ev Staples had found himself unable to finish his own "Holiday" costume because of working till the last minute on the costumes for the newest production number.

"You'll have to wing it alone," he'd said. A solo! "Improvise!" he had shouted at me. "They'll never know the difference!" I hadn't even had a chance to rehearse in the gown he'd made for me. He'd handed it to me at five o'clock that night.

Only half made up, I suddenly felt anxious and leapt from my chair to check my dress again. Was everything there? Underpants, shoes, gloves, veil, bobby pins (and safety pins just in case). I squeezed back into my place at the long makeup table. "Haven't painted my legs," I said aloud. *Finish the face first, silly,* I told myself. But I couldn't sit still. Pulling my robe up and sliding into slippers, I left the room and climbed the stairs to take a look backstage.

With nothing but work lights casting shadows from high in the flies over legs and battens, it was a dreary sight. The stage itself was still a mess of cables, and the crew, having dropped lighting pipes to waist level, were replacing gels faded by the heat of the lights during dress rehearsal.

I could hear the orchestra in the green room warming up—someone going over and over a tricky bit in the brass—someone else tuning tympanies. It churned me up. I remembered the way they had played "Holiday" last evening at full dress rehearsal. I'd never heard such excitement in the piece.

"I'll do it," I told myself. "I'll do it all right!"

"Half hour!" A voice over the tannoy repeated. "Half hour!" It must have been seven-thirty. My first entrance wasn't for over an hour, but I knew I must soon begin my warm-up. Back in the dressing room, I started on my face once more.

"Fifteen minutes to overture—fifteen minutes!" said the voice. That was Legrow. Or was it? Maybe Hozack? I was too new to the company to be familiar with all the NCOs' voices.

"Help me with the backs of my legs, would you, Stansell? No. Don't. You have a shirt on." The girls were half-dressed now, stockings and shoes, shirts. They would wait until the ten-minute call to put on skirts, ties, tunics and caps so they wouldn't get too hot. I hurried to finish and brush my hair up. Ev came into the dressing room to tie the net flourish on top of my head. "Knock 'em out!" he said. "You'll do just fine!"

I was dying to have a look at the audience coming in. I know better, but I love peeking at audiences, especially this one, which was said to include mostly important government and military officials from Ottawa. I also wanted to secure a spot in the wings where I could warm up and watch the opening.

"Break a leg, everyone!" I said, and once again departed the dressing room. Musicians seemed to fill every inch between me and the stairs. Someone I had never seen before told me to stand back. I did. Captain Farnon passed me on his way to collect his head-set from the stage manager and winked at me as he went by.

"Ten minutes to overture–ten minutes." Behind me, the dressing-room door opened, and as the girls pushed past me, the musicians made way, chatting familiarly with the women as they climbed the stairs. I followed in my dressing gown, and found a good viewing place tucked in beside the stage manager, Regimental Sergeant Major Don Hudson, near the head of the stairs.

"Five minutes–five minutes to overture." The wings were filling up on both sides.

Opening nights are always a bit nerve-wracking, but these artists hadn't performed for over four months and I could feel the quiet tension and excitement. A scuffle of shoes at the foot of the stairs told me the musicians were moving into place in the pit. A minute went by, then applause broke for Bob Farnon. I held my breath until the overture began. Big and brassy, sometimes marching, sometimes galloping, sometimes flowing silkily; always it came back to the strong-sounding march of soldiers en route with a lot of pride and optimism.

As the overture came to a close, the audience thundered its approval but Captain Farnon took no bow, segueing straight into fanfare for curtain and lights. The stage, set as a ship's side with smoke billowing from funnels, was a mass of flags and colours. A solid military song combined the crunch of marching feet with sixty male and female voices. These soldiers saluted the country, the job to be done, and the men and women who promised to do it. The scene had its sombre moments but it also included some neat inside jokes about army fatigues. An elite drill

squad did a few fancy manoeuvres as a reminder they really were soldiers, and then as the lights dimmed, the women sang about the unsung
heroes on the home front. Then flags, flags, flags against a blue, blue sky
when lights came up full again. There were, of course, boots–big, black
and noisy–caps to be thrown in the air and caught–whoops! Near miss
for the little guy on the end–as the troops completed the number and
marched smartly off. Left on stage were a couple of unhappy privates,
Shuster and Wayne, who ambled downstage as the curtain ran in fast
behind them. Applause. Applause.

The curtains re-opened on a canteen being cleaned by four privates
in overalls who did a neat drill with their buckets and mops. Enter the
hostesses led by Mildred Morey. Mildred could make anyone laugh and
was brave enough to make herself the butt of her own jokes.

Next, a spotlight revealed four elaborately mustachioed senior officers in a mezzanine box that literally overhung the stage, who fairly
dripped "red tabs" (the colour flashes worn by senior officers) and
scrambled eggs (the gold braid on the peaks of their caps). These four
were our male quartet–Sergeant Brian Farnon, Lance Corporals Ralph
Wickbergh and Denny Vaughan and Private Denny Farnon–who sang:
"On Behalf of the General Staff," written by Sergeants Shuster and
Wayne.

After a few more numbers, Roger Doucet, looking particularly dis-
tinguished in a white summer tuxedo, made his entrance to a burst of
applause. Roger's delight in singing, and his care for the words and
phrases he sang held special appeal for me. Listening in the shadows I
was doing *pliés*, touching my nose to my knees, putting first one leg, then
the other up a wall. I had to run downstairs to finish dressing so I missed
most of Doucet, but got back in time for his last offering. Now I
watched him from stage left, ready for my own entrance. He closed with
Gounod's "Ave Maria" with tears in his own as well as the audience's
eyes. They didn't want to let him go.

When my entrance music sent me flying in on the plucked strings of
"Holiday," my still-wet eyes must have sparkled. I was just
running–small, small steps at a fast pace–my arms spreading wide,

enjoying the breadth and depth of the stage. The repeat of the theme, an intricate piece of choreography, was easy to dance alone. Through the flowing bridge, I let the music take me where it would and, from there on, improvised with assurance. It was a holiday! I was free! And I had everything a dancer ever asked for–stage, costume, lights, a full house and music. I gave the audience everything I had, forgetting I was a soldier, forgetting I had no partner. The dress Ev had made was easy to move in, and behaved as it should, floating poppy-like and wrapping again. It did flip-flops when I made little jumps and clung when I was still. At the end, I did my deep classical curtsey and rushed off, knowing Bob was ready to bring his baton down on the intro to the next comedy act. But that was okay. I was in my own world and glowing. I knew I had done it all right.

I didn't stop running until I reached the stairs where I met the girls coming quietly up for their next entrance. Threading my way between the dancers I caught bursts of laughter from the audience and enjoyed the crazy bits of music Bob stabbed into the act presently on stage.

The second half opened with a number created by Aida Broadbent for Sergeant Hal Seymour and Sergeant Linda Tuero surrounding them with as glamorous a fan-production as you'd see at the Zeigfeld Follies. This segment had particularly delighted me in Vancouver. The dancers wore crinolined ball-gowns–flounces of pure white silk that actually touched the floor, hiding their feet as they moved quickly and so smoothly they might have been on ice–sixteen-button-length white kid gloves and headdresses made of tall ostrich plumes. Each carried a magnificent ostrich fan which, when held open with both her hands, was as large as her skirt. In a setting of black velvet, these full white fans caught the coloured lights that played upon the dancers as they moved, smooth as the silk of their dresses, from one breathtaking picture to another. The focus of each picture was the adagio team with their stunning lifts and spins. As Linda swooped downward from one of the lifts, her own fan started a ripple effect on the girls' fans which, paused in a high overlapping formation that looked like the crest of a wave, rolled outward until the fans spread across the floor as foam would on a beach. Having danced many beautiful designs, the girls finally mounted staircases, invisible to the audience against the black velvet backdrop, and arranged themselves into one gigantic skirt that completely hid the dance team. At this moment, Hal lifted Linda high aloft to create a china-doll effect above the skirt. Linda's last gesture was to place her fan behind her head as the whole skirt quivered in a cross flare of many lights. The curtain closed slowly on this magical display.

Soon enough, it was time for the Latin extravaganza, "Viva El Furlough." It exploded on the mainstage, taking the audience on a rhythmic and colourful South American journey. The only part of it I really recall was being front and centre in the spotlight, bending so far backward from a kneeling position that my head touched the floor time and time again as flying legs and ruffled skirts passed over me.

Freddy Grant's moving finale music filled the theatre for a full minute before the curtains opened upon a massive backdrop of receding hills with evergreen trees in the foreground. Above the sound of distant marching feet came the voices of the chorus singing "Let's Make a Job of It Now!" Then, in battle-dress and full voice, the CWAC singers and dancers marched in through the trees, making military formations before they formed parade downstage.

From high on the left of the hillside there entered a single file of soldiers wearing tin hats and carrying full equipment, including rifles slung across their shoulders. Singing as they marched, they criss-crossed the set via a series of descending ramps until the backdrop was completely covered with moving soldiers. As they reached stage level, the men moved forward through the trees to replace the file of exiting women destined to re-enter singly on the top ramp. The marchers kept coming and coming across the hillside until over one hundred uniformed soldiers were on stage. They sang their battle song from beginning to end over and over, as the audience stood up and joined the singing, standing and singing, marching and singing, "Let's Make a Job of It Now" until the curtains slowly closed between them.

Alicia Markova and Anton Dolin, stars of the American Ballet Theatre.

CWAC W 110-975 Private Sweeny, V., in Vancouver.

Top: Sports day for CWACs in training. I'm sixth from the right.

Right: Proudly, we display our summer uniforms. I'm in the middle. They weren't much good in Vermilion, Alberta!

Brand-new CWACs, trained and ready for posting.

Top: Sergeants Frank
Shuster and Johnny Wayne
were experienced and well-
known performers.
(National Archives of Canada,
PA 152119 [NAC])

Right: Flight Lieutenant
Norman Silk with a friend
in Calcutta.

Major Rai Purdy was slim and theatrically debonair.

Opposite top: CWACs with the Invasion Review perform in France.
(NAC, PA 132837)

Opposite bottom: Tenor Roger Doucet and baritone Andy McMillan
entertained Canadian paratroopers in Italy in 1944. (NAC, PA 152145)

Captain Maurice Bourque helping performers load a truck. Were those instruments "liberated?" (NAC, PA 211723)

CHAPTER 7

Onward to England

To everybody's great disappointment, our command performance turned out to be the last performance of the original Canadian Army Show. The very next day Major George called the company together to explain our new position. Although I had not been allowed to say anything, even before the command performance I had been aware of plans for dividing the company into five units. I already knew that units A and B were to be musical reviews, each to consist of a twelve-piece stage orchestra with solo instrumentalists plus a male and a female singer. They would also have one act, a couple of sketch characters and a dance team. Units C, D and E would have small (three-to-six member) pit bands, a line of girls, two comedians and some singers.

Now, after formally introducing the non-commissioned officers who were to take charge of each new unit–all familiar faces but some with new rank badges–Major George asked the production staff to describe how the new units would be assembled. Although he wouldn't be going overseas, Captain Brent joined Captain Purdy to explain formats for each small and intimate review. Felicia spoke for both of us about how we would steal parts of the present production numbers that could be suitably reduced in size and become the themes of the new units.

Each unit would feature one or more of the specialty acts who had agreed to go overseas–Comedians Shuster and Wayne, solo vocalists

Jimmy Shields and Roger Doucet, ballad singer Raymonde Maranda, and mezzo-soprano Mary Moynihan, comic Doug Romaine, magician Don Hudson, acrobat Ethel Hendry, actresses Gwendolyn Dainty and Lois Hooker, singer-comedienne Virginia Stansell and adagio dancers Linda Tuero and Hal Seymour. In addition, much fine solo talent had risen from the ranks, including singers Ralph Wickberg, Andy MacMillan and Uska Ollikkala who all had professional vocal programs of their own.

I was pleased to know that Ev Staples and I would finally perform as a team. When we learned we'd both been posted to B Unit with orchestra leader Sergeant Eddy Sandborne, we hurried to discuss music with him. Could he re-arrange "Holiday" for a smaller group? Could he ever! Eddy, a short guy with a big grin and blue eyes in a round face, was also a wonderful fiddler–he never called himself a violinist. He was really too old to be going overseas, but what a trooper he was!

It was a delight to be part of that little show unit. No one was the star. Every performer and every moment of the show was important to us. Ethel Hendry's specialty was an incredibly smooth acrobatic dance routine, performed to "Falling in Love with Love." Raymonde Maranda, our gorgeous French ballad singer, and Mary Moynihan, the symbol of wholesomeness, had always had requests for encores whenever they'd sung.

Every one of the boys in our band was a star in his own right–Teddy Rodderman (trombone), Pete Zamborsky (trumpet), Babe Newman (trumpet), Mike Barton (trumpet/viola), Pete Overhold (drums), Jim Coxson (piano), Lou Sherman (first violin), Frank Hosek (violin), Hank Rosati (tenor sax), Moe Weinzweig (alto sax), and Vic Bott (tenor sax). Putting them all together with Eddy Sandborn leading, we really had something much bigger than a twelve-piece orchestra.

Ev and I got a big lift from dancing "Holiday" and so, we hoped, would the tommies, able-bodied seamen and airmen for whom we would perform overseas.

For my second spot, solo this time, I repolished my favourite gypsy number. The wardrobe department produced a full peasant skirt with low-cut ruffled blouse and black laced bodice. I wore my own scarlet boots with their soft buffalo soles–old but so comfortable. And no one could make the gypsy music sound more inviting than fiddler Eddy.

Ev created "My Mama Done Tol' Me," for the two of us–a sleazy, sexy duo to music of the same name. For this, he designed a small, gaudy something-to-shock-your-mother kind of sheath, slit up one side. At first I was awkward. Ev must have died when I tried a slinky walk. "Wet your finger," he said, "and draw a line from your heel up the seam of your stocking." I did as bid. "Not like that! Feel the curve of your leg!" he almost snarled at me. "Take little steps putting one foot close in front of the other and let your hips move."

Though I still felt shy, I tried again and finally got the hang of it. I had never curled myself around anyone's body, publicly or privately, the way he was suggesting, but I'd seen apache dancers do it, and, with his continued coaching, finally allowed Ev to throw me about and drop me nearly to the floor, then grab me tightly to him and move as though we were glued. He was a good teacher, and I a willing learner. Had Mum seen the finished product, she would have dragged me offstage by the hair again!

With five new units to prepare, rehearsals went on in every corner of the theatre from early morning till late at night, with dancers from C, D and E units rehearsing on the stage by turn. While we each created some new work, Felicia and I stole everything we could from the big show, chopping and re-shaping production numbers whenever possible for fewer girls on smaller stages.

Between costume fittings, memorizing lines–we all did sketches–and military parades, our days were full. Outfitting for overseas also caused interruptions, though I was really glad to get my battle-dress and boots. The snug fit at cuffs, waist and ankles kept the wind out. Worn on top of our battle-dress, our greatcoats were wonderfully warm. With November well along, vaccinations and booster shots put some people out of action for a day or two also wasting precious time. We finally realized it wasn't possible to complete five shows in such an atmosphere of rush. The job would have to be finished in England.

Backstage activity increased dramatically in those early weeks of December 1943. Stagehands built massive crates, all grey with black numbers on them, and fresh shipments of makeup, mirrors and gelatine arrived daily. We knew our departure would be soon. I had learned that Norman was booked onto a ship bound for England and suddenly I realized how near I was to seeing him again. My happiness with these events precluded any comprehension of the sadness that the original members, having formed close bonds with each other, must have felt about breaking up the big show.

On a miserably cold December day, after a final parade of the whole company outside the Victoria Theatre, we women shouldered kit bags and slung haversacks across our backs to march the few blocks to Union Station. There, in the lower rotunda, endless tables displayed piles and piles of Red Cross winter underwear. We were halted, told to drop our loads and to stand easy near a rectangle of tables marked CWAC. As her name was called, each CWAC could choose several of each item in her size. When at last everyone but I had selected a bundle, it was discovered that although I had received promotion to the rank of sergeant two days before and the orderly room had struck me off strength as a corporal, they had failed to take me on again with my new rank. All the underwear that remained could hardly be called smart, pretty or even my size. Large beige woollies, knit on number-one needles with in-and-out elastics around the waist were the only things left.

"Oh, well," I comforted myself, "who cares what's under my battle-dress so long as it's warm?" Had we been warned to leave room for these items in our kit bags? I don't remember. I surely wanted to hide mine.

It was quite obvious when we climbed aboard our train that the CNR had put its most derelict passenger coaches back into service for us. The carriages were dark and the seats board-hard. During the long cattle-train journey to Halifax, we were given several half-hour stops for walks in the snow. We were warned to bundle up, and I recall feeling the dryness of sub-zero air in my nostrils. Now I was glad of my ugly woollies. Accustomed as I was to the soft moisture of coastal B.C.,

Seattle and England, Quebec's intense cold was new to me but exhilarating. I remember my delight, on one of those searing cold tramps, when I saw coming toward us a man in a little cart, his small pony with its frozen whiskers and an icicle beard, puffing along on stilts of packed snow. Together they made a picture that belonged on a Quebec Christmas card.

At dockside in Halifax we marched through one long, cold metal customs shed after another. Each had doors opening onto the side of a ship that seemed to have no beginning or end. Portholes and doorways, portholes and doorways. Finally our platoon arrived opposite a doorway where we were halted, stood at ease and told to drop our bags. We must wait our turn while endless lines of male soldiers boarded. When a reasonable space came between platoons of men–to the tune of cheery whistles from the fellows–we crossed a gangplank into a dark hole in the side of the ship.

Boarding a liner was not new to me–this would be my fifth Atlantic crossing–but sleeping nine to a cabin was. Bunks three high with barely standing room between them were only intended for lying on, not for sitting on. We therefore headed for the upper decks whenever possible. There, if lucky, we could sit on the deck or at least find a post to lean against. So as not to lose my place, I arranged to lend my post to someone else whenever I needed to walk.

The ship lay alongside the dock for the two days it took to load soldiers. Although all her identification had been removed, I recognized her to be the Cunard liner *Berengaria* which had brought me home from England–a sickly kid of fourteen–for an overdue tonsillectomy in the summer of 1936. Now the greyness of *Berengaria's* camouflaged hull was depressing, but it was even worse to find the ship's interior so shoddy. There were neither carpets nor chandeliers and there certainly was no music.

Thousands of us lined the decks on the afternoon of the third day when the ship moved out with small tugs straining sideways at the hawsers to get us free. The ship slipped away from the dock without any sensation of movement, but, though I'm sure everyone felt some sort of emotion about leaving Canada, we were all too cold to watch for long and headed for the lounges. Once the ship was faced in the right direction, the engine vibration told us the little tugs had been disengaged; we were steaming. Outside the harbour we slowed to a stop, and I felt the soft roll of open sea while more and more ships—tramp steamers and cargo vessels of all sizes—took their places in our convoy. Last of all the battleships, mine sweepers and destroyers positioned themselves on guard. By dusk, all portholes and windows had been blacked out, and though we knew they were there, the other ships became invisible.

It was late when we felt the engines throb again and knew we were on our way. By that time at least two sittings had gone through the messes. As the CAS CWAC platoon waited for our turn, we could feel the ship lifting and falling on a moderate sea. It was not enough to make the thought of food uncomfortable, but when our turn came, I was glad to sit on a chair in the mess hall.

Long after lights out, with all of us sergeants tucked in, if not asleep, I was wakened, as was everyone else, when the ship lurched and tipped sideways rolling us all against the wooden guard rails of our bunks. It was so sudden I nearly fell out on the deck. As everyone ooohed and ooowed, we clung to the boards for what seemed like several minutes before the ship righted herself and stayed level again. After the nervous chatter had died down, we went back to sleep, only to be thrown to the other side some time later. It was weird and scary, but since we'd been given instructions for emergency boat drill and there was no one outside the cabin shouting orders and no alarm bells were ringing, once the ship was righted, we mutually decided that these were deliberate changes of direction and nothing could be seriously wrong, so we stayed in the cabin and tried to sleep. We found out next morning that, owing to her greater speed, *Berengaria* had left the convoy behind; zigzagging was a way of reducing the risk of becoming a target for enemy submarines. Far from upsetting us, it gave us a thrill to think of ourselves racing across the ocean, outsmarting "Jerry." The ship did her best to roll us onto the deck every night of the crossing.

Safely berthed in Liverpool, *Berengaria* delivered up her three thousand-odd troops from what turned out to have been her own last safe voyage. During an air attack on the convoy with which she was returning to Canada, she was struck and sunk.

Meanwhile, along with thousands of other soldiers directed by provosts (British military police), CAS personnel were packed into dimly lit trains—the carriages well-worn and black window-shades pulled down—destined for Aldershot, an old military garrison town in the south of England.

After travelling all day, I heard my first "all-clear" siren as we finally detrained. "'Urry on there. Nuffink ta wurry abaat," said the provost to our platoon of Canadian women. "Tha's the end a tha' raid, a' least. You'll ge' used t'racket." We had been without sleep for over forty hours by the time the last CAS truckload of women arrived from the Aldershot railway station at the British Women's Army Corps (WAC) barracks.

Except for the sergeants, the women of CAS—now known as CAS Overseas or CASO—were billeted in several huts next to the WACs. Friendly and kind, the WACs had collected bedding from quartermaster stores and made up the bunks. They told us they had managed to scrounge fuel and had lighted stoves in the CWAC rooms to welcome us, but as often happened in those wartime days, our expected arrival date had changed, and when we finally turned up on Christmas Eve, those fires had long since burned out. It was just as bitterly cold in one of the WAC sergeants' quarters where Sergeant Linda Tuero and I were welcomed before we crawled—fully clothed but shivering—into a couple of spare, unused and therefore damp beds. We pulled our greatcoats over us as a last resource.

Next morning, although reveille—cheerfully played by a fine bugler with every note clear and strong—tried to blow me into a merry Christmas, I cringed against the chilly dawn that entered our quarters along with a sharp wind and chubby corporal Rosemary.

"Mewwy Cwissmus, hall yew lydees," shouted the jovial Brit in her best Cockney. "Hevewybody hup! Hive brought yew sum cowel."

Cowel was her gift of a precious, black, burnable substance, rarely available. "Jes' f'them Canucks an' cuz it's Cwissmus."

Because of our late arrival in camp and our enthusiastic welcome from the Brit sergeants, no one in our hut had enjoyed much sleep, so it took me half a minute to remember where I was and figure out why I had all my clothes on. With a sort of groan of "Thanks, Corp," I uncurled from the knot I'd been sleeping in and pushed my unwilling sock-clad feet to the floor. Staggering slightly on my still-wobbly sea legs, I pulled myself up to look around at the dozen or more women coming to life in pyjamas. I could easily pick out Linda Tuero as the only other Canadian in that hut because she, too, was fully clothed. We shot each other questioning glances as we slung on our greatcoats—mine had fallen to the floor—and dug out our toiletries to head for the showers.

Christmas 1943 didn't feel much like any Christmas I could recall. It was not quite raining but it was cold. Grey air hung damp between the old buildings as Linda and I asked our way to the sergeants' mess. We found it in a stone-walled, high-ceilinged building that echoed military boots and the clank of eating utensils on thick white plates. We marched to the end of the long narrow room to sit beside the only window. From there we could see other buildings but no sky. The place was almost empty. Did no one else eat breakfast? Those few who chomped re-constituted eggs on cold toast seemed not to notice that this was a special day. At home, even the dreariest roadside cafés would have had some tinsel dangling or some twisted crepe-paper effort to acknowledge December twenty-fifth, but no sign of decorations disturbed the bleak atmosphere here. I tried to remember if all Brits behaved like the Scots, ignoring Christmas, but making a hullabaloo about Hogmanay at New Year's. But instead, my memory took me home to my Canadian childhood, to the days before any of us had gone away to school.

I don't think Dad had ever missed being at home for Christmas when we were that young, although I know how difficult it was for him to make a living on "civvy street" after the First World War. Often he was forced to take jobs no one else wanted in places far away from Mum and his four children.

I particularly remember Christmas 1929, a year memorable to me only because I was seven, not because of the repercussions of the Wall Street Crash. It's true, we had been forced to move out of the Green Winter House on Barclay Street because my father could not find a job, and we took up rent-free residence in the Little House beside my maternal grandfather's mansion.

That Christmas holiday, Dad had taken my brothers, Sedley and Malcolm, who must have been twelve and nine-and-a-half, to Stanley Park to cut a tree in the forest. The three of them tramped home with their prize, a perfect Douglas fir about thirty inches high, for which Dad made a small stand that evening. It took most of Christmas Eve to trim this little beauty with a multitude of miniature trinkets hand-made by us children—painted macaroni chains and zigzag-cut silver-paper icicles. I remember thinking what a rich tree this was becoming as Dad gave us dimes and quarters, and even a fifty-cent piece, each to be wrapped and tied between the stars and sticks of barley sugar.

When we were finished, Dad asked us, "Who wants to come with me?"

"I do," the boys shouted and I copied them. Whatever my big brothers did was all right with me.

Sister Moira, not old enough to be out late in the cold, stayed with Mum. (Our youngest brother Roger wouldn't arrive for some years yet). Mother tucked me into my warm hand-me-down coat and did up the buttons. With Dad carrying the tree, we walked for several blocks before boarding a tram that took us to a part of town I didn't know. Then we walked some more till Dad stopped before a dark little house. He sent Sedley to knock on the door while he called out, "Hello, hello! Anybody home?"

The lady who opened the door peeked out as though surprised to have a caller. I could see a dim light behind her. "Hello, Mrs. Mallory," my dad said. "Perhaps you'd like a tree?"

"Oh, Mr. Ben!" She sounded as if she was crying. "Do please come in. Geoffrey will be so pleased to see you."

"Well, no, we won't all come in." Then to us he said, "Malcolm, you stay with Verity for a few minutes. Sedley and I will say hello to Geoffrey and come right back." And he handed Sedley the tree to carry.

Dad hadn't mentioned his plan to give our tree away, but we seemed to understand how two families could enjoy the same tree. There were no complaints. When they returned, Sedley told Malcolm and me that Geoffrey (Mr. Mallory) was sick in bed. And Dad explained to us about the "Old Contemptibles," ex-soldiers who had promised to care for each other.

Fourteen years had now elapsed since that Christmas, and with something of a thud my thoughts returned to the present moment. I took stock of the day and the mess-hall and truly understood the loneliness of all soldiers away from home. I had become one of them.

Except for Rosemary's burst of enthusiasm following reveille, that Christmas Day held none of the usual excitements for me. No hopeful glance at the bedroom ceiling to catch the reflection of fresh snow outside. No feeling of electricity in the air. No sitting in a warm bed surrounded by small edibles and ridiculous trinkets put into my stocking by Santa Claus. No music. No smell of cedar branches. No hope of a family gathering or even a call from home. No Christmas tree. No dreaming in advance the smell of onion dressing, or the taste of the bird itself, or afterward with a full stomach taking a walk or a snooze near a fire.

I was glad the bank opened next day so I could get cash for phone calls. But before my conscience would let me call Norman, I felt obliged to contact my father's sister, Doffie, the odd bohemian aunt under whose less-than-watchful care I had lived while studying in London. I didn't anticipate difficulty getting her phone number since I had her address, but there was no telephone registered to Miss Dorothea Sweeny. I should have remembered her boast that she had never paid tax here or in Canada and twigged that her house would not be registered in her name.

Next, with my conscience quieted but my heart thumping, I asked for Norman's number. He answered the telephone, "Silk here."

"Hello Norman. It's Verity."

"Sweeny," he said, then, "Hmm...hmmm!"

There was such a long pause that I said again, "It's me, Verity." I couldn't tell if he was glad or sad that I had arrived and I began to babble. "We got here on Christmas Eve. They made us welcome. I didn't have money for the phone, couldn't find Doffie. Are you all right? Can we...?"

He broke in, "I'm coming down. Where exactly are you?" I felt owned by the army and worried whether I was permitted to tell Norman, now a civilian, where to find me. Then he added, "Good to hear your voice, Sweeny." The sound was so suddenly warm I had no doubt he wanted to see me.

The world between our lives had been so vast it was difficult to believe I'd see him the very next day. I wondered how he would look, how we would greet each other, where we would then go.

Norman simply told me to ask for a pass and what few things to pack. He told me when to expect him and explained that he would take me home to meet his mother and father at the Mount in Widdington, near Saffron Walden in Essex.

I had stopped babbling. "Yes," I finally said. "Yes...yes..." And then he said something in Gaelic and hung up.

Next day, after tea, I stood beside a second-floor window that looked out from the ATS sergeants' mess over a parade square. Behind me, a dozen or so women sat chatting as I watched for Norman. Then he appeared. I'd never before seen him in a kilt though I knew he was accustomed to wearing it. He had sent me a photo at the time he joined the London Scottish and another of himself at home in Widdington playing his beloved pipes.

Bare-headed, he walked briskly, knee-socked and brogued, kilt a-swing, right across the empty parade square disappearing from sight behind the building where I waited. I don't think he saw me. He hadn't looked about him as he passed below the window. In the next thirty seconds I figured he should climb the stairs outside the building, enter, cross the hall and open the door on the far side of the room. I had but a moment. Should I remain looking out of the window, pretending I hadn't seen him, or rush to open the door for him? In the end I waited, turning only at the sound of his clipped and formal voice asking someone in the hall, "This is the ATS sergeants' mess, is it not?"

There was nothing odd about his speech to me then, but looking back I am touched by our formality, how few words we spoke, how emotional I was. And then I heard the doorknob turn. I crossed the floor, and when he had held open the door for one of the sergeants, entered himself and closed the door, I gave him both my hands. Straight-faced, we looked and looked, and then he grinned.

"Schlew!" he said under his breath. "I thought it might never happen." He had used his unique expression of wonderment, a word that was familiar to me from our earliest acquaintance.

Norman took me by the arm, guiding me back to the window. Reaching into his jacket pocket he produced a small black box. As he handed it to me he said, "Open it. It is yours." In absolute silence I did as I was bid and found a platinum ring with an emerald set tall and a diamond on each shoulder.

Looking back, I realize this should have surprised and shaken me. I should have asked important questions such as: Isn't this a little presumptuous? Shouldn't you have asked me to marry you first? Are you really well? What about my career? But I didn't. Just looking at this man, this long-time friend, I felt myself entering a safe place. I knew I belonged to someone at last.

With silent solemnity, Norman retrieved the box and took from it the ring. Carefully placing the box on the windowsill, he reached for my left hand and held it a moment. Looking at me as though questioning my response, he said, "I bought the stone in Calcutta. I hope you like it. The setting is platinum, the purest metal." I was captivated. Then he put my engagement ring on my finger and, ignoring all propriety, kissed me right there for all to see.

Coming back to this world, I searched for words to introduce Norman, now my fiancé, to some of the sergeants. They were all smiling at us. I told him how kind they had been in making us welcome. He thanked them also, then gathering my ready greatcoat and haversack, he hustled me away to catch a northbound train. I never did ask him how he knew the right size for my ring finger. He would only have said, "It was made for you."

We walked the half mile to Aldershot station, joining hands quite naturally although in our youth we had never been so familiar. I had a four-day pass. Norman was on leave—on sick leave, or more precisely, invalided out of the RAF—which was why he was not in uniform. Night had already fallen by the time we reached the station. The train was jammed but we squeezed aboard. Pressed against a grimy window in the corridor we held hands without trying to speak. No use shouting over the noise.

In the train out of London we found seats in a compartment. I leaned my head against his shoulder in the stiff old carriage and can recall long, speechless times while I savoured our new world. As ours was a civilian train, though almost everyone was in uniform, it often slowed and stopped for unaccountable minutes before crawling on again. In those war years, there was no assurance one could get from A to B within a specific time or by any recognizable route, but that was no concern of mine. Norman knew where to change trains, which we did several more times.

Well after midnight we walked the last mile or so from Widdington station to the Silk home where tea with scones and small sandwiches awaited us. Mum Silk was small and rounded and had warm brown eyes. Her smooth, dust-coloured hair, drawn back from a softly weathered, round face, was caught in a knot at the nape of her neck. In his particularly gentle way Norman introduced me.

"Dearest, this is Verity. We have come home." Norman's mum spoke a quietly lilting welcome, rather like a prayer. His dad, a small man whose silver beard matched his trim haircut, appeared from his study where he had been awaiting our arrival. Putting his two hands around mine outstretched to him, he made a formal little speech about having heard of me from his youngest son and retired again. As it was very late, quite soon Mum Silk showed me to my room. It was cold, but a stone bed-warmer had taken away any chill from the woollen blankets.

Although it was the very end of the year, the days I spent out of doors with Norman were pleasantly mild. In the daylight hours we walked in peaceful countryside, catching each other up on our lives since 1938. Of his two brothers and three sisters, all but his youngest sister Nan had left home, but he told me his mum always cooked up wonders in her warm kitchen whenever her children came home. The way Norman introduced me when his brother Colin and sister-in-law Beryl arrived to meet me touched me profoundly. Avoiding any suggestion that he owned me, he said simply, "This is Verity. We are going to be married." I already felt at one with this close-knit family.

I felt proud of Norman when he explained the labourious projects he had set for himself to bring his body back to health. He had begun weight-lifting by using a broomstick, which was all he could lift at first, then little by little had increased the weight until, "Now I can lift a great chunk of a tree-trunk above my head and do thirty push-ups," he told me joyfully on one of our walks, "and run half a mile!"

"Look!" he exclaimed as he drew himself tall and pulled his shoulders back. "I'm well and strong again. Let me show you." A twinge of anxiety struck in my gut. "Climb on that fence," he pointed, grinning. "I'll carry you on my shoulders!" His eyes twinkled and he looked ever so pleased, but I couldn't dispel the little fear that lurked between us, nor the feeling of embarrassment about trying to navigate a fence in dress uniform. I knew I mustn't discourage him after all he had been through, so I hitched up my skirt and climbed to the top rail of a wooden fence near the path where we walked. Then, holding the fence with one hand, Norman gave me his other hand to help me, most carefully, to sit upon his shoulders. With my heart pounding I put first one leg over, then the other, pressing my heels against his chest for balance.

Holding both my hands out in front of us, he walked head high with bold steps some distance along the path before I blurted out, "Let me down now. That's wonderful. That's truly wonderful." Like a child, he was so proud of his accomplishments and I should have been filled with joy for him, yet a bewildering mixture of emotions flooded me. He must have been terribly, terribly ill to have come to this moment in his life when he needed so badly to prove to me his capability. I didn't know how to look at him, how to give him reassurance, how to explain my sudden unbidden anxiety. I was talking pleasantries, at the same time thinking ahead and telling myself all would be well. No matter what lay ahead for us, we'd manage fine. I needed this dependable loving being who, like my dad, would always cherish me. This man had those same qualities I had looked up to in my father, that I wanted in my life again.

Although Norman had grown up in the Wye Valley in Wales, he'd been born and had spent his early years in Scotland, and he felt most at home in the Highlands. He spoke Gaelic and had taught himself to play the bagpipes. All of this appealed to me. The job he had held at Harrods when we first met had been something to make ends meet and to help his father keep the family home and allow his parents to live at peace in retirement. But even in those days, he had dreamed and talked of one day living in a shepherd's croft beside a Scottish loch.

As we walked, we talked about the future, and about his health. This did, at times, worry me. But Norman was straightforward about it. He'd explained that he would never take a city desk job, that he'd always have to exercise and work out of doors. To live in the country seemed reasonable, and though I'd lived in London and Los Angeles I had been happiest in bare feet at Pasley. Norman was well schooled and widely read. There'd always be plenty to talk about and he, too, had a great feel for the simple life. He loved folk music and legends. In our hearts we had so much in common. Wasn't that the most important thing?

Since he was not employed, he returned with me as far as London, giving us valuable extra hours together. By the time we parted there, I felt thoroughly at ease with him.

While I convalesced at Alderbrook, Norman, back in uniform, managed to visit.

CHAPTER 8

Sirens, Bombs, and One Nasty Fall in Guildford

Scattered about in temporary billets the members of CASO company, having no designated meeting place in Aldershot, had experienced great trouble finding each other. When our adjutant raised objections, the company was allotted a collection of ancient brick buildings on the outer edge of the garrison. Condemned as useless for at least fifty years but still used in a pinch, the buildings were in considerable disrepair and obviously had not been occupied recently. Their quartermaster signed us in and we set to work, like friendly Canadians, to make our quarters habitable. No, we didn't need carpenters, thank you. We had stage carpenters and scene builders. Yes, we could clean walls and floors and the women knew all about cleaning windows. The larger assembly rooms became rehearsal halls, kitchens became laundries. However, we couldn't pretend we were very comfortable with draughty doors and windows that didn't fit. The stone doorsteps had been worn into curves and the bricks had crumbled on either side. Marks remained where shelves had once been, and nails or holes showed where pictures had hung. We scrubbed them or painted over them, but hide them we could not. However, within a few days we had our section in shape and we set about completing the shows.

While no unit used a piano in actual performance because they were too cumbersome to carry around, each of the five shows had a piano lead-sheet for rehearsal. When word went out locally that CAS needed a couple of pianos for rehearsals, the call was answered within days, and after tuning, these instruments weren't bad at all.

Before issuing a rehearsal schedule for dance routines, I called a warm-up class of limbering and stretching for all dancers. Although we had been on a number of route marches for exercise, none of us had danced for over six weeks, and it felt good to be in practice clothes again. Bodies that know how to work can't help working hard, and we all complained of stiffness after that first class. Since their dancers were soloists, A and B unit used Hall 2, the smaller space, leaving Hall 1 for C, D and E units' chorus. Counting opening and closing numbers plus at least one other production number in each of those three units, there were ten or more pieces for me to work on as choreographer. Three rehearsal calls a day gave each unit an hour and a half to warm-up and practise show material. At first the routines looked awful. I felt sick to see such confusion and sloppiness, but we were all so glad to get back to work, the precision returned in no time.

As long as the units were to remain in southern England, one of the things it was necessary to practise was spreading out—or squashing in as the need might be—to fit the performance venues, every one a different size and shape. Once out in the field, we looked forward to using our own fully equipped eighteen-by-thirty foot portable stages plus two TCVs (troop-carrying vehicles) backed in, one on each side, to provide wings and dressing rooms. These stages, fully equipped with curtains, legs and battens, could be erected almost anywhere.

Because most air raids came at night, blackout was in effect from dusk to dawn all over the country. All windows had blackout drapes, all doorways had additional black curtains a few feet inside and there was always someone on duty checking for chinks that might be visible from overhead. Everyone had been issued a flash light but we were not to use them except in emergencies. My unusually good night vision gave me an advantage, but my shoes suffered like everyone else's, the backs of our heels quickly becoming rough from feeling our way off curbs.

The drone of planes overhead was a constant reminder to take precautions. The locals as well as the service people who had been there any length of time could recognize each type of aircraft by the sound of the engine or the whine of the prop. It could be a Lanc, a Welly, a Spitfire, a Yank Liberator or a B-17–"one of ours" returning from a mission. But it might be a Jerry 1-11 or DO-17 coming in high on a long flight, and we knew someone would "cop it" far up north when darkness fell.

The high troop concentration in Aldershot, where CASO was billeted made us a natural target for their raids. Although there was always the sound of shouted commands and platoons of marching feet and the roar of troop carriers and tank engines around Aldershot, when the raids were on, ack-ack and sirens added to the hubbub. The ominous wail of the air-raid warnings, up and down, up and down again began most evenings just after dark. There must have been a siren on a building very near our barrack because the wail was almighty loud.

At first the sirens terrified me, and each exploding bomb sounded as if it was right next door. But we learned from the locals. They simply remarked on who might have got it this time, or said something like, "'ello, 'ello, 'ello?" and carried on. It was a while before I could adopt such a casual attitude. We newcomers were shown where the air raid shelters were–"That brick roof beside the parade square covers the stairs down, and there's another across the street, see?"–but although I made a note of where they were, I never actually went down into a shelter. It seemed more trouble than it was worth to run for cover every time a siren wailed.

After a warning we wouldn't always hear the plane or planes, and sometimes the all clear sounded without anything else happening. If the guns near the coast "got the bugger," we escaped. When a real raid was in progress, the ack-ack fellows would trace the incoming planes. Sometimes we'd hear the warning, hear the ack-ack and maybe hear the bomb explode. The all clear might sound for only a moment before the warning came again. On a bad night the sirens often overlapped. There wasn't much we could do except know where all our people were and follow orders.

I can see myself now on such a night in Aldershot–full of authoritarian bustle, greatcoat over pyjamas, tin hat hanging off the back of my head–checking my brood as they crowd into my small sergeants' quarters, propelled according to orders by the wail of the sirens: uuuup...dooown...uuuup...dooown.

I itemize their equipment: "Blanket, greatcoat, respirator and tin hat–OK! OK! Squeeze in! Make room! Come on in! Who's missing now?" The wailing siren is joined by the dull thud of ack-ack guns some distance away. Excitement and nervousness keep the incessant chatter and insistent questions at a high decibel.

"How long does this go on?"

"How do you know when it's over?"

"I'm going under the table!"

"Stay away from the window!"

"What's the drill, Sarge?"

"Hey! What's that noise? Who's shooting who?"

Moments later, an unholy crash not far away.

The realization that all is well on our patch breaks the tension. Very soon comes the steady note of the all clear.

"Holy Dinah!"

"Wow!" and a dozen other exclamations.

"Who got it?"

"Is that it? Can we go back to bed?

"I'm cold."

But another warning takes over from the all clear and we know we aren't going anywhere. I lift my voice. "Where's Shepherd? Where's Hendry?"

Laughter and chatter about fear make it sound fun, but the wail is clearly saying "Here we go again!" just as the two missing girls arrive.

"We couldn't find your room."

"What the hell was all that?" Chatter about how they threw themselves under a bunk when the crash came. Much laughter. Someone says she grabbed her rosary. Another, a picture of her boyfriend.

"You're supposed to come down here!" I shout. "Where's Dainty? This may go on all night."

"She's coming!" And in bursts Gwendolyn Dainty, blond hair flying, arms full of stuff. Pushing through the others she dumps herself and her stuff on my single bed already piled high with respirators and tin hats. With a thundering crash the bed collapses, giving the girls their nastiest fright so far. For a moment no one speaks. Then a hell of a screeching and screaming erupts, tears and laughter mixed.

They were so young and so brave without knowing it.

Meanwhile, back in Toronto, CAS had remained active although they had moved out of the Old Victoria Theatre. In their new quarters, a small show factory developed, and CAS staff gave regular auditions for performers, who were then sent to be inducted into the army. After two months basic army training, they'd spend four weeks learning a new show. Well before Toronto sent over the first new unit, they shipped us a lot of costume accessories such as hats and shoes, boxes of makeup and the always welcome practice clothes they knew we couldn't get in Britain. At that time we had no extra storage space in quartermaster (QM) stores, which was already crammed with an assortment of oddities such as straw hats and dancing shoes in addition to the standard uniforms and toiletries. As a result, the new stuff was dumped into the smaller rehearsal space which wasn't big enough for its purpose at best.

This overcrowding, plus the fact that the British mess halls were several blocks away and their meal times didn't fit ours, prompted the adjutant to ask that CASO be relocated. As a result, the whole Army Show got marching orders just as the first five show units were ready to go on tour, and the unit tours had to be postponed. Frustrated, we packed to move the whole company, administration as well as barracks, to a new location.

Changing quarters was not exactly like moving house, although both are emotional experiences. No one had to worry about the van.

There was no furniture to transfer. No one paid the light bill or arranged to change the telephone number. When orders were posted, the wheels ground, and everyone did a super cleaning-up job. The CWACs returned their bedding to QM stores—they would pick up another load on arrival at a new destination—and when the trucks came to remove them, they were waiting with everything they owned in two kit bags, a haversack and a purse. Slung across their backs were canvas satchels containing their respirators from which dangled tin hats and metal mess-tins.

We were all ready to climb aboard the troop carriers when word came that the barracks we were leaving had not yet been inspected for damages by British army authorities. What we didn't know was that in taking over these barracks, the Brits would mark down every chip of stone and brick, every nail hole and the several cracks in windows that had been there before we came, while our own officers had failed to do the same when we had taken over. Now to our surprise and fury, the Brits had the gall to charge these items against us. With the compliance of our own adjutant, the privates and non-commissioned officers were ordered to pay barrack damages of several hundred pounds. And it was pay up or suffer punishment. Our officers nearly had a revolt on their hands, but since they apologised to us for not having noted the rough spots when they signed us in, we forgave them and forked up from our pay books.

CASO's next home was a small village on the outskirts of Aldershot called Ballydieg. Set on a bit of a hill, it was the first part of a civilian housing development which had been commandeered by the army at the outbreak of war. Its several streets of small, newish houses had white picket fences and even a little landscaping. A small parade square was surrounded on three sides by mess halls, rehearsal rooms and an orderly room. The officers' mess was close by. We thought we were in heaven.

There were drawbacks, however. Nice as the houses looked—each room with a fireplace, three beds to a bedroom, a downstairs sitting room and a huge concrete tub over a wood-burner in the laundry room—the big problem was going to be keeping warm. We didn't find this out immediately; for a whole week we enjoyed making fires and laughed as we learned to use the old fashioned wash tubs. By the time we remembered that fuel was rationed, we had used up a whole month's supply of coke. We also learned that gathering around small coal fireplaces is the quickest way to get chilblains, those itchy red swellings caused by putting freezing-cold feet too close to direct heat. And we all got them!

Our adjutant acted as though we should have known about rationing, and he posted a notice telling us that if we wanted a fire, it was up to us to go through our dustbins and pick out half-burned coke. Some of the men, however, took things into their own hands, and very soon the picket fences and even the boardwalks began to disappear. No one was blamed.

One of the really weird British army orders specified airing of blankets between 0900 and 1100 hours. Though the month was only February, we were required to comply every Tuesday. The fences had disappeared, but there were still some bushes and, damn it, out went our blankets rain, fog or frost. Was it any wonder most of us caught colds? To make matters worse for our health, the women's platoon was always sent onto the parade ground ahead of the men and had to wait in the bitter cold. We women used every method of rocking and toe-wiggling learned at basic training to keep blood circulating. Eventually, when our chilblained feet would no longer fit into shoes, we were allowed to wear only socks inside overshoes on morning parade. A sad-looking lot we must have been!

The first new unit from Toronto was F unit. This group was to follow in the footsteps of units A to E which, having performed in all the local bases, would soon be shipped further afield. When they arrived in England, all the new young people had to go through the excitement of raids and near misses, of travelling in the dark and of catching colds as we had all done before them. Their show units had been put together loosely in Toronto and needed polishing, plus the addition to their scripts of appropriate current political or military jargon. But as choreographer, my greatest problem became not having enough time to recover from one set of colds before the next batch of CAS recruits engulfed me with their coughs and sore throats.

But CASO was quite settled in at Ballydeig and I was healthy by the time Norman came to get me. He had recently passed a medical and talked the War Department into reinstating him. Now stationed at Hartlebury in Worcestershire, he once again wore the blue uniform of an RAF squadron leader. No one would have known, seeing him walk tall and straight toward me, that he'd ever been ill. I knew it, and he knew it, but today the world could see him at his most handsome now.

When he came to take me away that Friday, it was not to go to his parents' home, but to be alone together. This, in my mind, meant long walks and talks and shared meals. We set off in high spirits. The CO told me later that as he watched us walk away I was so glowing that he had no doubt to whom I belonged.

Neither Norman nor I had been given any sex education by our parents except to say that we should live "happily ever after" with the one we loved. Mine had explained nothing about the strong biological feelings connected with reproduction and, so far as I could figure things out, nice people didn't even think about it. Norman, on the other hand, had made a point of finding out about the habits of men. He firmly believed in the rightness and beauty of healthy sexual relationships and he shared his thinking with me. Even in this wartime setting where casual affairs flourished everywhere, there remained an assumption between us that our relationship was not like that. It was in fact extraordinary that a delicate, formal, controlled romance such as ours should have blossomed. I don't believe it could happen now. Looking back, despite all the travelling I had done, I realize that I continued to hold exceptionally old-fashioned and romantic views on what made a woman a lady and a man a gentleman. Norman understood and honoured my feelings.

He had chosen a small hotel just a couple of train stops away from Aldershot. It was an old place on a river with its own water wheel. Not expecting to be in the same room, I gulped when he said he'd sign us in as man and wife. "Isn't it illegal?" I whispered. He put his arm around my shoulder, assuring me I needn't worry. We climbed the stairs and followed a dimly lit corridor. When we came to our door, I stood back while Norman, his cap tucked under his arm, unlocked it and held it open for me. I walked past him and crossed the wide floor to where a greenish light spread into the room from a small window. As I stood looking out through leafy branches at the river, I knew Norman waited for me to turn to him; and when I did, his eyes filled with tears. Concerned by this intense show of emotion, I looked away.

Then, when Norman unbuttoned my shirt, dismay engulfed me as I caught sight of my dreadful woollen Red Cross underclothes! It hadn't dawned on me, dressing that morning, that he and I might stand before each other without clothes.

As I relaxed and became less awkward with him, Norman showed me the scar on his ankle where some farmer had actually shot him with an air gun when, as a boy, he'd been caught poaching rabbits. He pointed out, too, the place in his groin where a medic in India had sliced him to remove a cancerous lump. The word stung. I tried to dismiss the feeling of fear that cancer conjured.

That night we lay in the same bed enjoying the warmth and closeness, but we didn't make love. I am sure Norman believed, as I did, that intercourse should wait until we were married. Though I felt far more at ease with him the next day, most of which we spent discussing his understanding of sex, he continued to hold his calm. "There's lots of time," he promised, "and we'll be together for all the rest of it." That evening Norman returned me to Ballydeig.

When Units A to E were finally ready to take our shows on the road, our first performances were fairly local. The units followed each other on a circuit, playing nightly to packed houses of service people in all the gymnasiums, local theatres and drill halls within a radius of twenty miles of Aldershot.

The weather that spring was wet, cold and sometimes foggy, and since we travelled mostly at night, driving was particularly traumatic for the Canadian MT drivers who had to map-read by flashlight while driving on the left-hand side of very narrow roads. The headlights of our vehicles had been painted over, leaving only the barest of slits aimed no more than six feet ahead on the road to avoid light being seen from above. The sound of planes overhead was a constant reminder of the danger.

Like the men, we women travelled in open trucks, oftentimes with curlers in our hair, but in uniform nonetheless. While travelling, we sang variations on popular marching songs or chattered in a series of new 'languages' which were all the rage in 1944. "Pleazese peazass theaze cresazackers and cheeazese" or "Herve yer sern mer ner blerd-stern rerng, Erbert?" (Have you seen my new bloodstone ring, Herbert?)

When B unit got to where we were going, we found no proper dressing rooms. Quite often the women had to run outside and into another building to change costume. Coming off stage in a sweat after dancing with Ev, I either flung a greatcoat over my shoulders or simply flew out into the night and the rain to the dressing room. But I flew a few times too many and deepened my cold into pleurisy. When I complained to production officer Captain Purdy about the awful conditions, he said I should wear a dressing gown. Since I'd lost mine, left it in some dressing room, he lent me his. Nobody warned me I shouldn't have accepted—a sergeant doesn't borrow officer's clothing, especially a dressing gown.

The longer CASO stayed in Britain, the further afield from Aldershot the first five units played. The shows had been well received locally and requests to see them now came from stations all over Britain. As a result, the first five units moved out to billets in pubs and hotels in the Midlands, taking with us all our personal gear. From these locations each small convoy visited a series of regiments and squadrons within a radius of fifteen to twenty miles. The routine was simple. Early in the day the technical crew delivered sets, lights and costumes, put in a stage if necessary, and hung the show. In the evening, TCVs delivered the performers in time to take care of chores such as setting up dressing rooms, mending and ironing.

B Unit's first foray away from headquarters was to a base in Nottinghamshire. Our billet was a baronial castle on the edge of Sherwood Forest. Cold and forbidding as the stone walls made it, I could imagine Maid Marian held captive in a tiny room off one of the spiral staircases, and I felt the presence of the Merry Men in the near-by forest. For a week we remained there, shivering for lack of heating fuel. It was to take many months before our Canadian blood thickened enough to cope with the interior dampness of British billets.

Next we moved to the Barley Mow, a famous pub near Dorking in Surrey. It was already familiar to me—not that I had ever been there—but my English sister-in-law, Diana, had written me that I should look in the massive guest book for her name and that of my brother Sedley. They had honeymooned at the Barley Mow four years earlier.

When Unit B moved into this billet, as sergeant in charge of CWACs, I was given a minuscule private room. For the first time in my life I slept in a feather bed, and under the quilt my feet met a hard, warm something which, I now recognized as a bed-warmer. It gave me a feeling of comfort, indeed luxury, that I hadn't expected.

As senior NCO, one of my responsibilities was to see that the three CWACs in my care, Corporal Raymonde Maranda and Privates Ethel Hendry and Mary Moynihan, got enough exercise in lieu of parades and route marches to keep fit and out of trouble. Privates Hendry and Moynihan chose to walk, but since this was riding country, I went look-ing for horses. By the second morning at the Barley Mow I had con-vinced Corporal Maranda, our ballad singer—who had only ever ridden a pony at a fair—that she would love to ride with me.

I had found a nearby stable willing to rent us a couple of hunters. No doubt, I thought, our pounds sterling would be a bonanza to the stable owners whose rental business can hardly have flourished late-ly—there being little or no hunting during the war. Of course, we had no riding britches, but our battle-dress and brown army boots would do fine. Hatless, we tramped off across wet fields on a bright late March morning, avoiding as best we could the remnants of the previ-ous night's surprise snowfall.

My flamboyant description of having ridden to hounds as a young-ster in Scotland probably encouraged the stable owners to rent us their most spirited animals—out of condition, but nonetheless capable. I bounded onto my horse. Corporal Maranda accepted some assistance and allowed the owner to adjust her stirrups. Asked if we knew the roads, I looked toward the top of a cliff bright in the morning sun and said, "No bother. I can find the way." A bit embarrassed that I'd for-gotten how to gather my reins, with elbows up I rudely kicked my mount out of the stable-yard ahead of Raymonde. For a half hour or so we walked and trotted our horses side by side along the road without incident. At first Corporal Maranda made a noble effort under my instruction to post at the trot—that is, intentionally rising and sitting on alternate strides to avoid bumping in the saddle. But she had to give up, resorting to the sitting trot as one does in a Western saddle. When she seemed comfortable and in control, I led the way up a steep lane toward my goal. This entailed passing under a dripping stone bridge which didn't please the horses, but, at my insistence and using our heels and a lot of encouragement, we pushed them on and on.

As the ground grew steep and quite rough, I kicked and pushed my horse harder, although this was obviously against his will. I began to complain about the poor shape the horses were in, but as long as I could make mine move, Maranda's horse followed obediently. I was determined to reach a point where I was sure we could get a clear view of the beautiful countryside. In fact, we did, and it was glorious. For a little while we rode about quite relaxed on the plateau, enjoying the sun, the sky and puffy white clouds. Looking down from our hilltop, we could see bright green patches of a golf course showing through the melting snow.

When it was time to head back, the story changed. Those beasts knew they were going home and they also knew the shortest possible way. They'd had enough of us and made no excuse for their rush-and-tumble descent. With Maranda's horse now in the lead, they slipped and slithered their way down all the steep banks we had labouriously circumnavigated on our ascent. Cantering across a very wet field, they simply took us where they wanted to go, which ultimately led along a high stony embankment beside the golf course. No longer content to canter, Maranda's mount shook its head, grabbed the bit in its teeth and took off at full gallop with my horse in hot pursuit. Hauling back on their mouths had no effect whatsoever. Maranda, with her arms and legs flying, yelled back at me: "I can't stop him!"

"Neither can I!" I shouted at the new leader, hoping to give comfort as well as to show I wasn't afraid. I called ahead, "We might as well let them go. Just enjoy it!"

Finding a pony's rhythm and staying close to it when it is on the rampage is scary but wonderful. Faced with similar fears during my adolescent years, I'd had some of my best rides. So now, taking courage, I settled down for the bolt. The gravelly road, the pounding of hoofs, the flying trees and the pounding of my own heart are clear in my memory. I can recall, too, the brilliance of reflecting puddles and our splashing through them. I clearly remember the exhilaration along with guilt for having invited Maranda into such an adventure.

She was far ahead of me when my horse shied, dumping me into a puddle. I remember seeing Maranda approach on foot tugging her reluctant horse by the reins. When it saw me, it yanked away from her and fled. She pulled me from the water onto some grass. I recall vomiting, and Maranda telling me she must leave me to find help, but at this moment, like some miracle, a bobby on a bicycle happened by. The next thing I recollect is lying on a bed while Maranda's hand stroked my forehead. My head hurt and I asked for a pillow. She could have explained that I already had a pillow, but she didn't.

"I think my foot was caught in the stirrup," I babbled. "The horse's hoof must have hit my head as I fell. He shied at a puddle. I'm all right. I'm quite all right. I'll be okay in a minute...in...okay...in a..." My voice trailed off. No longer the bumptious CWAC sergeant, I lay still again, on my soiled pillow, mud-streaked and sopping, much to the dismay of the brave corporal who had gone riding with me.

"They wouldn't even allow me to wash her face," I later heard Maranda saying. Owing to army regulations, I could not be cleaned up in any civilian cottage hospital but must wait for a Canadian ambulance. The two Canadian medics transferred me face down onto a stretcher and covered me gently with an army blanket. Then moving carefully through the narrow doors and corridors of the little hospital, they carried me to a waiting vehicle.

The journey was long and tedious, more than thirty miles to a Canadian hospital. Fortunately for me, I was unconscious most of the way. Since I had a CWAC companion, the two medics rode up front. Regaining consciousness periodically, I was aware that my head hurt. It felt as though my face was banging on a board. Again I begged for a pillow and again passed out. Each time I awoke, Corporal Maranda spoke soothingly, stroking my muddy hair away from my very pale face, avoiding, as best she could, the bloody mess at the base of my skull.

When next I came to, Maranda was gone. There were men around me. I could hear their voices but could not distinguish the moving shadows. I felt hot and uncomfortable and tried to throw off the cover. By then, though I wasn't aware of it, they had removed my soaked clothing. I was naked. Laughing, they tried to keep me covered. My head hurt. Why couldn't I have a pillow? I passed out.

Nearly a week went by before I opened my eyes again. Still unable to focus, I heard the shadow at the foot of my hospital bed say, "Schlew!...so you've come back!"

Norman explained to me that while I was unconscious Captain Purdy and Lieutenant Lineaweaver had visited and brought mail from members of the company. Since I couldn't see, he read me letters from my companions in B unit and the telegram that Mum had sent, full of optimism, from Vancouver. He said Lieutenant Lineaweaver had spoken of returning to Canada. He also gave me other news he had learned from the visiting officers about changes in rank and position back at CASO HQ. All of this I promptly forgot and had to be reminded of later; but the information did gradually filter through to me that I had been in an accident, suffered a basal skull fracture and been on the critical list for ten days.

Next day—and the next and the next—Norman was there, as well as my Aunt Doffie, who had moved into a nearby pub so that she could look after me. She brought messages from all her/my friends and showed me the oranges she had collected from their ration cards. Wasn't I a lucky girl? I forgot the oranges as fast as I forgot everything else. My Aunt Doffie came and went. Norman seemed to just be there.

I didn't wonder yet about B unit, but when I did, I became desperately concerned that my hair wasn't set. I must get up and get dressed. Somehow I must get to the performance. I must! Norman told me I wasn't going anywhere for a while.

Slowly I recognized the doctors and interns who surrounded my bed each morning. Every day they asked me the same questions and told me their names yet again. I could soon identify the one who said he was Dr. Stuart. It was he who told me I must behave and cooperate or they might have to help me along with an operation to remove a blood clot lodged in my brain. I began to anticipate their regular visits because of the needle they plunged into the base of my spine to draw the blood from my spinal column. In the end, it took several of them to hold me down because I couldn't control my shivering when they did it. For seven days I had that spinal tap every morning and it must have worked because at last they said I wouldn't need the operation. One after the other and day after day, the medics continued to prod. They scratched my diaphragm and the soles of my feet with the point of a pin, but I appeared to have positively no reflex actions. Then they searched for clues in my eyes. I learned that I was a guinea pig for Dr. Stuart, a famous Montreal brain surgeon, as he taught his medical students. This became more embarrassing for me as my eyesight returned.

When one day, to remove stitches, they took off the sticking plaster skull-cap which had covered the back of my head, I discovered that area had been shaved. How my short hair prickled on my pillow! By this time I was able to sit up and could brush what was left of my unruly coif. I could actually see Norman now, and despaired the sight I must look to him.

Then, the day came when he had to say goodbye again. "They'll toss me out if I don't get back to work soon." And so I was left with Aunty, huffing and puffing from climbing up hospital stairs and navigating the long corridor. She didn't enjoy looking after me, nor did I enjoy her caretaking. My forgetfulness annoyed her, especially when she found that I hadn't remembered to eat the oranges she'd brought from her friends' ration cards. How ungrateful of me!

In time I could remember that I was at the military hospital at Basingstoke in Hampshire, west of Aldershot. I learned it was Canada's number one neurological unit, and that the entire staff of the famous Montreal Neurological Hospital had volunteered for service and had been moved here as a team. They dealt with head wounds, burns and plastic surgery, accepting casualties from all the Allied forces. They treated us with tenderness, patience and loving care. I shall not forget friendly and long-suffering Major Stuart, nor Sister Hilda Bossy, who never brought me a bedpan that hadn't been warmed.

The Basingstoke Hospital was on a private estate lent to the Canadian Government for the duration of the war. Entered through huge doors at the head of a broad staircase, the mansion housed administration, admitting, X-ray, and operating rooms. The wards were Nissen huts placed end to end until they were eighty feet in length and attached to the mansion by corridors, dull black tubes like the arms of an octopus. The wards had concrete floors and small windows, but they were relatively easy to heat and the Bakelite floor tiles shone from diligent waxing and polishing.

I was the only woman patient at Basingstoke but I learned something about the men patients from the night orderly who became quite a good friend. When he came on duty each midnight he checked the men's ward first, then if I was awake, he'd spend some time with me, bringing me the odd treat, such as fruit or a biscuit.

When I was sufficiently recovered, the doctor decided I should go visiting in the adjoining ward. For weeks I had listened to the chatter of the men's voices, and sometimes heard them shout to each other or to the orderlies. The afternoon orderly wheeled my bed into the corridor with me propped up against pillows. Although the lights were brighter there, I still couldn't see very well and suddenly felt shy. As we entered the men's ward, dear Sister Bossy came to my rescue, introducing me first to Big Jeremy who winked at me and gurgled. He couldn't speak.

Sister Bossy told me where Jerry was from, about his family and how he came to be there. I'd already heard that he had thrown himself on a grenade, saving several other chaps. Both his hands were gone, but they were rebuilding his face which was presently in a sort of metal cage, a bit like a character out of *The Man in the Iron Mask*. Jeremy's hair was blond, his eyes blue, his shoulders broad and he looked awfully young. They said he would make it because he was such a good sport.

The orderly pushed my bed on, and Hilda introduced me to Tom, telling him I was a dancer. She said Tom had been in an airplane crash. He was obviously badly burned. Most of his face was bandaged and his blankets were pulled up to his chin so I couldn't see whether his chest and arms had been burned too. Tom made a joke about being afraid to meet girls unless he was in disguise. They moved me on again and parked my bed across the ends of two others where the occupants were less distressed. As she left, Sister Bossy said she'd fetch me later and I quickly learned how gossip travelled there. All the boys seemed to know what had happened to me. They asked me about the Army Show and told me about themselves and others in the ward, especially about Peter who occupied the bed surrounded by curtains. They said Peter was Royal Navy. Blown up at sea, he'd lost a chunk of his head, he'd come to Basingstoke because of Major Stuart, the same wonderful brain surgeon who was looking after me.

Everybody knew that the major was doing his utmost to save Peter—a seven-hour operation one night and back on duty next day. Since Peter had been magically put back into working order, it was heartbreaking to learn that Peter had developed a mastoid infection. For days we all prayed for Peter. We thought he could...but he couldn't.

My afternoon visits became a ritual, with the patients who could speak shouting hello as they wheeled me in. Later, when I could walk,

I made my own rounds to see how they were doing. Judging by the cheerful banter on the ward, a visitor from elsewhere would never have guessed there was a war on except that every bed was filled, and some had curtains around them. Death was close for a good few, and others were so strung up, so bandaged and patched together, I wondered how there could be joy of any kind in that place. Yet, of all the friendly, cheerful and optimistic environments I've ever been in, Basingstoke stands out. Churches ought to be like that. Some of the boys would never go home, and some would go home unrecognizable, but their spirits had been nourished in a way that could carry them far in the lives that lay ahead of them.

When the day came for me to dress and go outside, the orderly returned some of my clothing—not my CWAC uniform, but my underwear and boots and a blue overall, the uniform worn when patients were well enough for walking out. Of course, when thrown from my horse I had been wearing those Red Cross charmers, my hand-knit beige woollen vest and pants. As with all personal clothing, my mud-soaked undies had been boiled in the hospital laundry, and as a result had shrunk so small they wouldn't have fit a teddy bear! What's more, they had cut me out of the vest so now it opened down the front. Suddenly I saw a picture of myself being undressed upon my arrival and remembered throwing off the blanket. And here I was, the only female patient among all those men, and they must know all about my horrid underwear. Such an embarrassment! However, I kept those historic items and later used them for polishing my boots.

On my first day outside, I met Jim who said he'd be glad of a partner for ping-pong. I accepted with glee although I was still cross-eyed and we both were very wobbly. Jim's jaws were wired together, and he had to take his food through a straw that fit into a hole between two teeth. He giggled when he told me through closed teeth how he sometimes forgot and tried to stuff a biscuit into his mouth.

Uncoordinated though we were, Jim and I had a laughing good time falling over ourselves to fetch that miserable ball. We almost never managed to return a serve, but on that day I learned that you don't have to be perfect when you meet on equal terms. And it came as a gift at last to be able to look fearlessly straight on at disfigurement and let it be. I had been told as a child never to look, never to stare, always to "leave at peace"—as my mother would say—anyone with an affliction. Of course, that was in the period following the First World War when so many men of my father's age were legless, armless, eyeless. We children knew we were lucky that our dad had escaped with only a couple of wounds. The one in his hip we never saw, but there remained lumps of lead from shrapnel in his bumpy hands, although he could still make them play the piano with great gentleness.

It took a long time for the medics to recognize that I had totally lost my sense of smell. After three weeks in hospital, my pleurisy and colds having subsided, they tested my nose over smells such as coffee, peppermint and ammonia, none of which registered for me any longer.

Everyone hospitalized for a head wound, the other patients explained to me, was required to have his brain photographed before leaving the place. The procedure was called encephalography. The details they described were gruesome to say the least. Nowadays, there's nothing to it, no pain whatever, but in those days the same type of needle they had earlier inserted into my spine to remove fluid was also used to pump oxygen up the column into the patient's brain. This was done with the patient wide awake.

When my turn came, not without anxiety but feeling pretty fit, I put on my hospital gown and walked beside an orderly to the operating room. There I climbed up onto a high table about the width of a stretcher.

"Sit facing the other way, your back to us, dangle your feet over the side. That's right. Take off your gown." I hopped down, removed the outer layer and swung onto the table once more. No use being afraid. They would do what they would do and I would survive. After all, I knew the routine. It wouldn't be fun but I was prepared—I thought.

When they had untied the strings of the inner gown I felt cold alcohol being applied to the base of my spine. Another breath or two, then two hands held my shoulders and the needle went in. Earlier, when they'd done the spinal taps, they had sometimes hit a nerve when they stuck that needle in, but not this time. I could hear the rubber tube being fixed to the oxygen tank and felt it being attached to the needle. I heard the metal knob on the tank squeak when someone opened the valve, and I felt the first bubbles of air and oxygen rise up my spinal column and plop into my head. It came quickly. The pressure made it feel as though my head would burst.

"No more! No more!" I tried to shout, but I heard nothing. They held my hands when I wanted to hold my poor head but they didn't stop. My ears blocked. My bulging eyes saw nothing but red. I couldn't scream. I couldn't think clearly. Still the pressure increased. This is craziness. *I'm going mad!* was all I could think.

"Breathe," I heard someone say. "Keep breathing." I tried, but I lost consciousness—woke again when someone slapped my face. "Breathe. Breathe." But I must have sogged completely. Next thing I knew I was on my back retching, retching. I left the scene again. They slapped me again. I woke retching. "Breathe! Don't go to sleep! Breathe!" they shouted at me. I kept passing out.

When the X-rays were completed they must have let me be. Next thing I knew I was on my side in my bed with a head so terribly sore I couldn't move, so hot it felt on fire, so big it felt like a pumpkin. I didn't open my eyes. What seemed like a very long time passed, coming to, fading out. One time I woke to feel many hands from my head to my feet lifting and turning me and gently laying me down on my other side. It was excruciatingly painful. I didn't move until they came back a long time later to turn me again and again, all night and all the next day. I never saw them. When I woke from a long sleep the pain was less. I could see and I could move my body. I could manage to turn over but it hurt, and the bubbling noise in my head was extraordinary because every time I changed position, the bubbles had to get to the highest part of my head.

My experience was every bit as horrific as the fellows had warned it might be. Although the excess oxygen did gradually become absorbed, it remained for at least a month. Even after I returned to CASO, I still experienced some after-effects. Having lost my sense of smell, everything I put in my mouth tasted metallic and I thought my fillings must have rusted. The taste of rotten tomatoes and petrol pervaded all food, an unpleasantness that lasted for several months. But the worst moment came when preparations were in progress for an expected gas attack from the Germans and I realized that I would not be able to detect mustard gas by its smell. I remember panicking after hearing some small explosion. Suspecting the worst, I held my breath, went rushing down a corridor to throw open a window to stick my head out for a safe breath, only to remember that if a gas bomb had exploded it would be outside, not inside. I must breathe! But how could I? I had left my respirator behind in the office. Momentarily my own panic had frightened me.

After discharge from the hospital, I was sent for six weeks of convalescence to Alderbrook, a beautiful estate that had been lent to the Canadian government by a British family as a quiet retreat for service women on sick leave or awaiting passage home. The gardens were extensive and old. Meadows carpeted with spring flowers spread among giant oak and beech trees. Several times during my residence there, Norman made the complicated journey from his station at Hartlebury to visit me. We both gained strength that spring, and spent many hours wandering by streams or sitting in the grass enjoying the peacefulness and making plans for our future. On one of those visits Norman told me he had bought the shepherd's croft in Scotland he had long wanted.

The Tin Hats—female impersonators—were consummate professional entertainers. (NAC, PA 152148)

CHAPTER 9

Invasion Review Performs Under Fire

I n May 1944 the doctor said I could leave Alderbrook
Convalescent Hospital. Since I was only a sergeant, I had
expected that the new CO, Major Purdy, might send a car for
me, but instead he came himself to collect me. I vaguely wondered at
this, but I was preoccupied with what lay ahead.

As we set out, he explained that CASO HQ had moved. This time
it was to Camberly, a rather posh small town just outside the bustle of
Aldershot garrison area where there were picturesque officers' schools
and officers' messes. Then, as he drove, the major briefed me on the
various personnel changes that had occurred since I'd been away.
Captain Farnon, he said, had become head of Canada's music broad-
casts from London. Major George had moved to London with a raise
in rank, leaving the position of command to him. Some of the older
officers had returned to Canada, and although he didn't go into details,
Major Purdy explained that because he had received notice regarding
the infringement of standing orders of one of our units in the field,
he'd had the unfortunate task of demoting and disciplining two
NCOs, Shuster and Wayne, whose promotions to warrant officers he
had earlier supported. He said he had sent the whole unit back to
Toronto.

Several original units had returned to England, he continued, and more new ones from Canada were making their first local tours. I was dying to ask "What about me?" when he finally mentioned that he had arranged to attach me to headquarters as permanent choreographer.

Then Major Purdy dropped his bombshell. According to an Army Medical Corps memo that he had received, my head injury automatically lowered my service category to S (for stability) and forbade further overseas travelling. Although the hair on the back of my head had grown in, and my shortened haircut disguised my accident, in light of this ruling I could no longer dream of dancing again with my unit outside England. In any case, following my accident, Ev Staples had found himself a new dance partner and they had gone to Italy without me.

The major went on to explain that my first tasks would be to organize the refit of two of the original units due back shortly from Italy and to polish another new one coming from Canada. Since Lieutenant Lineaweaver had gone home, and the acting CWAC officer, Audrey Shields, would soon be leaving, he suggested that when the immediate choreographic jobs were done, it would be time for me to take officer training in Aldershot. After receiving my commission, I would also be expected to take on responsibility for CWAC discipline and quarters.

Upon arrival at CASO HQ, I discovered that some kind soul had packed and moved my belongings to the new base. I found my kit bag and my few personal things next to a bunk in the sergeants' quarters. Most of all I wanted to dig out some practice clothes and find a place where I could work, but I was dismally disappointed by a further memo from the medics ordering me not to dance at all for at least two months, and never again to perform in a show. When, fresh from their tour in Italy, my old buddies from B unit came into camp at the end of July, I was suddenly filled with jealousy. There seemed nothing left of my once-promising dance career.

However, at our first business meeting when Major Purdy brought me up to date on the production situation and told me his plans for the units in for refit, I began to see that I was needed. As soon as the new arrivals had been through their physicals and taken a short leave, I called dance rehearsals to refresh and tidy up routines that were to remain in the shows, and discussed with their NCOs ideas for new material. The dancers were happy to work really hard and have a critical eye on them again, and it did me a power of good to feel my own creativity rise.

As well as dance numbers, numerous singles and acts were to be refreshed. Virginia Stansell, a singer and dancer with home-grown talent and home-grown vivacity had been picked up by CAS out west about the same time as I was. Stansell had marvellous dark eyes, black-lashed and naughty. Her hair, shiny black with a coppery tint, was wavy and quite wild, and her wide mouth smiled a lot, flashing gorgeous teeth. She had risen to solo status at the time the big show was split up in Toronto, and when her unit returned to camp, it was fun working on a new version of "Milkman, Keep Those Bottles Quiet." Virginia's kooky sense of humour made her great for sketches.

Then there was Ron Leonard, a master magician who did his tricks with such aplomb one had to believe in magic. But even if he hadn't done them so well his act included the luscious Pearl Sanders who was so beguiling it was hard to keep one's eyes on Ron. He certainly had class in tails and top hat.

An incredible impersonator, Doug Romaine came by his talents naturally. His father was Don, one of the original First World War Dumbbells. Doug used his voice to take his audience car racing, golfing, sky-diving, riding a bronco or anything else that was suggested to him. Scrawny, big-nosed and fast-talking, he made absolute magic with a microphone. He also could be counted on to turn up unannounced with hilarious one-liners throughout his unit's show.

Within a few weeks of my return to work, three small, well seasoned, all male entertainment groups joined CASO at Camberley. Drawn from particular Canadian regiments, they had been performing in England long before CAS arrived. They were organized on the format of the Dumbbells which, back in the First World War, had been the prototype of Canadian service shows or 'concert parties' as they were then called. Some of the performers with the groups that came to Camberley—the Tin Hats, the Kit Bags and the Haversacks—were veterans from the original First World War units. Like CASO, the units had also toured in Canada before coming to England, but unlike our family-oriented, review-type shows, the language these fellows used was coarse and their humour ribald.

The Dumbbell-type concert parties were like soap operas with permanent characters. Since there never had been any women in the shows, part of their unique attraction was the brilliant use of female impersonation. With the Tin Hats company came two impersonators, privates Bill Dunston and Johnny Heawood. My memory of young Johnny is of a dynamo—fast, funny and smart. Although a crack rifleman, he played the epitome of the "blond bombshell" and was a skilled dancer. It was fascinating for many of us in CASO to be this close to these consummate artists, to watch them painstakingly apply their makeup, and to see how diligently they dressed their elaborate wigs and cared for their elegant gowns and jewellery. We admired their professional and slick acting. The songs they sang were never far from blue but still terribly clever, revealing the influence of Noel Coward, then at his peak of popularity in England. A regular performer at the Stage Door Canteen in London, Coward was always generous in providing new material for artists in troop shows.

From financial and administrative points of view it made sense to combine these three concert parties with CASO. As well as feeding, bedding and shaping them up on parade, the Army Show gave them space to rehearse and let them get at it. They also had the use of our costume, music and scenic departments and could dump the responsibilities of travel, billets and pay on our orderly room staff. Pride, however, caused the odd flare-up between our performers and theirs. Although these concert party people had originally been trained as soldiers and wore Canadian uniforms, once they became entertainers, they had not been subjected to army discipline as we had. They resented our parades and brass polishing; our people felt they got away with murder—which they often did!

In addition to the concert parties, numerous small groups of British civilian show people belonged to an organization known as ENSA.

They had been 'doing their bit for the lads' since the very beginning of the war. But trying to manage without government support, with poor set and costume facilities, next to no money, and nowhere to rehearse, it wasn't surprising that many of these concert parties had become grubby and lax. Not being regulated as we were, they could accept invitations to party in the messes; as civilians why shouldn't they? But perhaps this is why CASO went overboard in the opposite direction and came away with a squeaky-clean reputation. Although there were over ninety CWACs on strength, CASO had only one illegitimate pregnancy and very few reprimands for sloppy behaviour.

For the protection of our CWACs, all our units had been sent on tour under the supervision of non-commissioned officers who could stay close to their charges day and night, especially after they left England. CASO's standing orders gave the highest authority to a unit warrant officer, which meant that his word was as important to members of his unit as any command from a brigadier general who might—and sometimes did—order the CWAC members to report to the officers' mess after a performance. When this occurred, the unit warrant officer, without apology, returned the women to camp, usually a barbed-wire enclosure with tents, dug latrines and a soldier guarding the gate with a gun.

The other major difference—besides our clean reputation—between CASO and other entertainment groups was that Army Show unit personnel did all their own 'set up and strike' chores. It was not unusual for a CASO unit to be met on arrival at a military or other station by a fatigue party expecting to lift and carry and help in any way they were needed. Although the civilian groups—and even Canada's own Navy Show—accepted this kind of service, it was not so with our units. Any fatigue party was immediately dismissed by the CASO warrant officer.

Once at a performance site, with the vehicles in position to provide the wings, the men from the unit bolted the portable stage together and hung the curtains. When the PA system and lighting equipment were removed from the trucks, the women set up the dressing rooms there, and unpacked and pressed their costumes. CASO had every reason to be proud of the way their entertainers handled themselves in the field.

As well as performing groups, representatives of Canadian service clubs such as the Knights of Columbus, Lions and Kiwanis came to England to make the lives of service people less lonely and more comfortable. They wore uniforms with *Canada* on their shoulders and were attached to CMHQ, but they had a tendency to turn up their noses at regulations. One of them was Captain Bob, the liaison officer between CASO and the Red Cross, who became known as Ask-Uncle-Bob. It was through Ask-Uncle-Bob that the Red Cross gave us patchwork quilts for the girls' bunks, and it was Ask-Uncle-Bob who found and brought us a supply of wonderful British boots—womens' army boots—for all our CWACs. They were gorgeous, well-fitted, high-laced, brown English pebble-leather, and they polished up like silk. I wore a pair, too, and I have to admit I didn't question the rightness of it.

It was because of my working relationship with the CO that I learned about Bob, who, being stationed in London, knew where to get extra cigarettes and liquor, how to arrange compassionate leave, how to get hotel rooms for officers and tickets for the theatres. Bob loved his association with CASO and visited us at every new location with goodies under his arm. He also enjoyed the welcome he always received in CASO officers' mess and drank until late with the best of the men.

Having been away from CASO so long because of my accident, I hadn't expected to be granted leave in a hurry. However, early in June I was permitted to spend my twenty-second birthday with my cousin Maureen at Pickhill Hall, her home in Wales. During my dance training in London, we had enjoyed each other's company on many holidays, but this was my first chance to see her in nearly six years. Much had changed in our lives. Neither of us was on the front line but we had both been immersed in the effects of the war. At eighteen, Teen—the nickname she liked—now served with the Land Army. Had the war not intervened she would have been a debutante. Still, she was engaged to marry Roddy Owen, a handsome Guards officer.

Both of us were aware that a turning point in the war was expected as soon as the build-up of Allied planes and equipment was sufficient to launch an offensive. But on my birthday we didn't want to think about it, and we climbed to sit on top of a huge haystack, the old-fashioned kind that had its own scaffolding and roof. There we talked about remembered Easters and Christmases, and especially the summers we had spent together here in Wales or at Maureen's grandfather's home in Scotland. Together as children, we had swum in cold rivers, explored rabbit warrens, plucked chickens with the scullery maid, folded sheets with the laundress, and, joy of joys, ridden ponies (later horses) over open countryside.

That day, June 6, 1944, as we sat in our hiding place atop the hay, I was in uniform, my brown tie removed. Beside us, a portable radio was tuned to the BBC which was giving a continuous report of actions along the English Channel. Although we chatted merrily about all the people we had loved or loathed, we kept one ear open for the important announcement that had been in the offing for so many weeks.

Then, suddenly, there it was. The radio announcer shouted, "D-Day has arrived! The long-awaited Anglo-American invasion began at sunrise today." Then came the recorded voice of General Dwight D. Eisenhower, Commander-in-Chief of the united forces: "Allied naval forces supported by strong air forces began landing Allied armies this morning on the northern coast of France."

As the Americans delivered more aircraft, British planes became available for night-time air raids over the Continent. Luftwaffe raids over England began to declined as their fuel supplies were cut off. But in July the Germans launched single, rattling, pilotless planes called V-1, which carried high explosives. These 'bombs' were aimed at specific targets. If one heard the thing, one prayed for it to keep going. When the measured fuel supply ran out and the noise stopped, the plane simply crashed.

The Shuster and Wayne group, together again after a protracted leave, back in Canada had been enlarged and rebuilt as *Invasion Review*. Frankie and Johnny were still the stars, but the unit was touring with two new warrant officers in charge. Although they were great performers, it had been a mistake to expect these two to also handle administration.

By the beginning of July a million troops had landed in Normandy and we were informed that *Invasion Review* was there with them. Not only that, quite by accident, *Invasion Review's* slightly off-course convoy had liberated a village. When the bouquet-carrying citizens cheered them and clambered onto the vehicles, our boys did a quick about turn, but it was too late, they were already heroes. Word quickly got back to us that the show was a smash hit with its ridicule of the German high command and daring portrayal by Shuster and Wayne in appropriate costume and makeup, of the two nudnicks at the top, Hitler and Goebbels. The effect of the laugh-filled show on weary Allied troops was like a tonic, and the ever-changing audiences lapped it up, hour after repeated hour, as they paused for a breather from heavy fighting.

We never saw the show back in England but the story of *Invasion Review's* adventures following the troops on a long, long tour through France to Esquelbecq in Belgium and to Nijmegen in the Netherlands, performing almost non-stop at times during the tough, last battles right up to and following VE Day, would make any Canadian proud.

At Camberly we began to hear outgoing daytime raids and sometimes saw planes heading toward the English Channel. Though a plot by his own generals to assassinate Hitler had failed, it was general gossip that once enough Allied planes were available, one gigantic raid would erase Berlin.

But the Germans were not quitting yet. The next missile to attack Britain from sites across the channel was the V-2. A much more accurate enemy—but silent; if you heard the explosion, you were still alive—which accounted for five thousand British civilian deaths.

With no hope of seeing each other for weeks, Norman and I kept in touch by letter and the occasional phone call. Meanwhile each of us requested permission to marry from our own branch of the services. In those days, as well as filling out a lengthy form, applicants were required to report to a military hospital for a physical examination. I felt so well I knew I'd pass. Except for having lost my sense of smell, there were no longer any residual complications from my accident.

A few days after I'd handed in my request, I reported to admission and was directed to gynaecology. That I must submit to an internal examination came as a shock, but even more upsetting was that, as a teaching hospital, two of the three people examining me would be students. Most Western women alive today have endured this invasion of private space, some often enough to have built up defences enabling them to endure the discomfort and embarrassment of it, but right then I felt humiliated and reacted with anger. Who gave them the right to trespass? How dare they?

In late July, I was ordered to attend an interview at officers' training school. Having accepted me into the CWAC without formal education—my formal education had been discontinued in favour of full-time dance studies when I was thirteen—the authorities were now accepting me as a trainee without the necessary education to become an officer. However, I knew all about standing orders and dress and drill, so my studies were to begin with army law and focussed on the orderly room procedures to do with charges that might be levelled against CWAC personnel. I had learned most of it at basic training, except for the obvious change in point of view. After half a day in Aldershot, I went back to CASO with some books to study and a memo to return shortly for another interview to be followed by my written exam. The whole thing appeared to be a formality which hardly interrupted my rehearsal duties.

From then on, becoming an officer was a bit of a lark. My main job in the Army show had always been choreographic, but since no one in army HQ had any knowledge of choreography, Major Purdy was obliged to ask me to produce a list of appropriate questions for the examining officers in Aldershot to put to me. I also supplied an answer to each question for the examiners. My next chore was to remember what answers I had supplied them and make my own responses just different enough that they wouldn't suspect our bluff. It worked.

Within a month, I became an officer with the lowly rank of sub lieutenant: I had one shiny brass pip on each shoulder. Since I was still in the same unit where I had been an NCO, there were awkward moments. Ways of addressing and saluting turned upside-down for me. Although in the officers' mess I could now call the chaps by their first names, I found it difficult to do this in the rehearsal hall; "Major Purdy" or at least "sir" seemed more appropriate. Besides returning the salutes of other ranks, I had to continue touching my cap to officers senior to me, though no one of my own rank. I became fixated on the red tabs worn by senior officers on the epaulets and collars of their uniforms. Once, when on leave in London, seeing the red tabs of a "big shot" approaching along Regent Street, I went into a flap. Flattening my hand as I raised my right arm to shoulder level, I formed a tight fist at the peak of my cap. I'm sure I went scarlet! But I soon got the hang of it.

At Camberly, trying to cope with two jobs, choreography and CWAC administration, I had more than enough to do, but within a week of becoming an officer I was relieved of some of my duties by the posting to CASO of a strictly administrative sergeant, Mary Sullivan. Sully, who was quickly promoted to staff sergeant, stood tall and expected the most from everyone. It was delightful for me, as a fledgling officer, to be able to lean heavily on her. No longer did I have to try to cover all of my CWAC's daily needs; Sully filled me in on how the women were behaving, what medical and clothing parades they should go on, who needed special attention and care, who should have compassionate leave and who should be smartened up. Sully and I got on really well; in fact, she gave me some of the mothering and companionship I'd forgotten all about, having been on my own for so many years. We all loved her even though she was strict and insisted the women in her charge turn out immaculately.

All that autumn of 1944, each time a unit came into camp, Sully and I inspected the CWACs, quartered them and took care of their personal health and welfare. I remember an occasion when we marched a group of weary women, just returned from Italy, to their new quarters. Proudly I showed them some recently acquired bunk beds covered with cheerful quilts from the Red Cross. I expected the women to be impressed. Exhausted, they flopped onto the quilts, grubby battle-dress, boots and all, obviously too tired to notice. Sully didn't reprimand them; she simply invited them to empty their duffle bags onto the floor so that we could decide what needed to be thrown out and what could be salvaged and laundered. An upside-down kit bag is not the tidiest sight at the best of times, but when the last item to exit is a couple of inches of sand, one can guess the owners have recently been in a hot and dusty place. This bunch is headed for hair washes with Lysol, I told myself, no question of that.

The clothes in those kit bags bore no resemblance to the uniforms they'd left with. This was all stuff picked up from a variety of QM stores—summer drill shorts, desert boots, brown kerchiefs for covering curlers, more brown kerchiefs for covering noses and mouths. But there was an order to it. I learned that these strange uniforms had been carefully chosen and approved by the warrant officer who had done his best to keep his company cool and clean. The women explained that the Army Show convoys in Italy were always required to yield to armoured vehicles and troop carriers. This meant driving the show convoy off the road as far as possible time after time to allow urgent traffic with its inevitable cloud of dust to rumble past. The unpleasantness of the scene wasn't difficult for me to picture, but I still felt a twinge of envy.

Italy had been the destination of several Canadian Army Show units early in 1944. I learned that except for some Canadian nursing sisters, the women of B unit had been the first female Canadian soldiers to land in Naples and entrain to a small town near the front where their quarters were a bombed-out building with only half a wall between them and a casualty clearing station.

Another unit, very close to the front lines, had to drive under an umbrella of heavy mortar fire aimed into enemy lines in order to get to the site where they were to perform. Once the stage was set up, the firing ceased. The audience rode in on motor bikes and parked on a hillside to watch the show. When it was over, the soldiers returned to their gun emplacements and the show packed up post haste to get on the way to their next engagement before the barrage opened up again.

Back in England, where at all times some CASO shows toured, even with the best of good intentions a show could lose its sparkle because of tiredness, poor dressing rooms, awkward spaces in which to perform, awful weather or simply taking things for granted. My job was to put the sparkle back. Some love and smartening up at home base did wonders. If I could help it, no one would say about our show people what I said about many of the ENSA show people and other civilian entertainers.

But it was more difficult to keep control outside England. Once a show left for overseas, it toured three months, and occasionally more, depending on the size of the war zone. While mobile, it was up to the NCO in charge to keep the cast in shape, insisting on physical exercise, especially for the dancers.

As each unit returned to England after a tour, they dumped their grubby costumes, went through medicals and left the noise of Camberly for two weeks leave. That was when our head of music, Tony Bradanovich (who was known in the music business as Bradan), Rai Purdy and I put our heads together to create a whole new production for their next tour. When Rai and I had decided on a theme, Tony brought us a selection of music that focused on our ideas, and then we sat down with costume designer George St. John Simpson to discuss wardrobe for production numbers. We went through the same thing with the set designer who would supplement the unit's curtains and 'legs' (the battens that separate the stage from the wings) with several portable set pieces. Rehearsals began as soon as the troop came back from leave. As an actor often played many parts, there were many costume changes. Working from our rough outline, it took approximately four weeks to rehearse and costume a new show and put it back on the road.

The CO and I decided to re-group all the tallest show girls together in E unit. I found it great to choreograph kick routines for them because they had such lovely long legs. Since they weren't cute or quick, I had to compromise by using music that had twice as many rhythmic beats as the girls actually used. This gave them twice as much time to make extra high kicks and to make fan kicks that were enormous. We had fun syncopating and emphasizing off-beats in the music, and because they liked what I was giving them, they did it well. Of course, with their height these show girls looked wonderful in feathers and in slinky gowns too. Though we never intended them to behave like Follies girls, they looked surprisingly glamourous.

Gwendolyn Dainty was one of these long-legged beauties, but she also did a telephone sketch called "Maisie." Dangling a leg over the corner of a desk, massive amounts of blond hair falling in her face, Gwen would carry on a one-sided telephone conversation that was so inept, inane and hilarious, she would have to insert long pauses to wait for her audience to quit laughing. While she waited, she used her eyes to carry on the comedy. As soon as her audience stopped laughing, she'd roll her eyes again. It was ever so simple, but she cracked them up every time. I'm sure her famous harpist father, Ernest Dainty of the Toronto symphony, would have died if he had seen and heard her.

Invalided out of the RAF, Norman was able to come to see me almost as soon as I'd arrived in England.

CHAPTER 10

For Love and War

In September, hardly three months after my own recovery and return to CASO, I received a memo, delivered by the CO himself, telling me that Norman was in the RAF hospital at Cosford in Yorkshire. Recently, he had written about several horrendous headaches; now I learned that during his morning pushups a blood vessel had burst in his brain. X-rays revealed a brain tumour.

Major Purdy told me to go at once and stay as long as necessary. At his suggestion, the orderly room provided maps and timetables, and a warm staff car hurried me to catch the four o'clock at Camberly station.

The first train went as far as London where the wait was only an hour, but the evening was chilly, as it often is in England in September; I wished I'd worn my greatcoat. To complete the journey I had to change three more times during the night. Once, as I stood shivering on the dark platform waiting for a connection, the station master pointed to an empty train that was, he said, the one I wanted but not due to leave for three hours. Though the passenger doors were locked, he showed me that the windows were not, and he helped me climb through one of them so that I could curl up on a seat in a lightless carriage and sleep until the train was ready to pull out. It arrived at Cosford around noon the next day.

The town of Cosford is famous for growing lupins, and there they were by the thousands in every colour, many of them over my head. The grounds of the hospital were planted with nothing else and I walked for what seemed miles between rows of lupin, across what may once have been an airstrip, to get to the hospital building.

Norman lay flat between unrumpled sheets in his pristine private room, waiting for me. He managed a smile of sorts and taking my outstretched hand spoke slowly. "Sorry, Sweeny, I hadn't counted on this." His mouth was dry. The words came with difficulty. Those beautiful dark curls and his strong mustache emphasized the whiteness of skin pulled tight on chin and cheek bones. He was freshly shaved, but the blue of his beard showed through. His eyes, half closed, were sunk deep under heavy brows. My heart ached as I kissed his parched and sticky lips and spoke softly about how he'd soon be well. "I'll come again and again to see you, as you did for me. You'll see. You'll get better as I did. And when this difficulty is passed, we can get on with planning our lives." Sometimes he closed his eyes just listening. Sometimes he tried to respond–a word or two or a pale smile–and I'd tighten my grip on his hand. From somewhere I summoned cheeriness, remembering the beauty of his letters as he had made dreams for us.

I was offered a bed in a chilly nurses' hostel reached by a long flight of exterior stairs, and I did sleep there for several nights. My days were spent with Norman doing what I could to help him with meals, giving him mouth washes and bathing his eyes. I tried to read to him but that seemed too impersonal. So I just sat, thinking up things to speak about that might keep him believing in our future. He hadn't much energy to spare me. However, after almost a week I felt guilty about staying too long, and knowing I was also needed at the base, returned there.

It was three weeks before I went again to Cosford and crossed the airstrip with its lupin sentinels. Norman was waiting for me in a wheelchair.

"Take me for a walk, Sweeny. I'm getting better. These chaps know what they are doing."

And so for several days I walked, pushing the chair up and across and down the lupined pathways, straight lines in all directions. And I remember how, wrapped in blankets and strapped into the chair, he had laughed—a thin sort of coughing sound—at himself, at his condition, at life. It made me want to cry. A bleak wind blew across the airstrip, making the lupins lean.

The weather had grown more cruel the next time I went there to be of comfort to my ailing love. The once-grand lupins now depressed me. Proud and unbending, the lupin can take a lot of wind but when the broad green stems become woody and brittle, some of them break like shards and point sharply downward, while the rest, flowerless, still point skyward, pretending. Overblown in September, faded in October, I no longer thought them beautiful.

When in November I came again, Norman wasn't so well, so we stayed in his room. With the help of his brother Colin, he had managed to arrange to have my wedding ring there. It was a circle of diamonds set in platinum. I loved it. He asked if we could be married very soon. Of course, I agreed. My permission to marry was due any day. I let him place the ring on my finger and he said, "Take it. Wear it. It is yours." As had the emerald, it fit perfectly.

In uniform one doesn't wear jewellery. Aware of that, Norman had given me the fine platinum chain on which my engagement ring already hung from my neck. Opening my shirt, I put the two rings together, hiding them away for the time that should soon come, perhaps right here at his bedside.

But two days later when I left, walking away between tattered brown rows of lupin toward Cosford station, one hand holding the strap of my haversack, the other clutching the two rings under my shirt, I think I knew I would not see my man again. The cold reached my bones and there would be no heat in the carriages.

In the garden around the officers' mess in Camberly, hoar frost, like trillions of icy needles bristling in every direction, disguised each twig and branch of yesterday's black and shiny trees. The late-November air was dry and fairly crackled, prickling the nose and catching in the windpipe. Stiff grass crunched under my feet.

There would be no more treks north to Cosford. Yesterday the CO had informed me that Norman was dead.

I trod on round the little house, noticing the untrimmed vines leaning in stiff arcs away from windows and downpipes. In peacetime someone would have cared for that pretty country cottage. At present it housed a handful of Canadian officers. Since my commission had come through, I had been eating there and spending my evenings with the men though I slept elsewhere. I felt detached, other-worldish. There was nothing I could do now for Norman. There was nothing to look forward to.

I made one more journey north. Norman's father, his brother Colin and I attended the stiff and impersonal RAF service for Norman. Afterward we took his ashes to the family home at Widdington. Mum Silk told us Norman had asked to have his ashes scattered over Ben Nevis, and this she later arranged with the CO of the RAF station in Oban, Argyllshire. I have the letter to Norman's mother from Squadron Leader John Logthis confirming that he had fulfilled her wish.

Many, many years later, with the sadness of my long-ago loss still asking for closure I wrote "Full Circle."

> This is a poem for my love
> Scattered though his ashes were
> Over Ben Nevis
> In our youth.
> Long are my years,
> Yet warm the dream we shared
> Of shining-haired children
> Kilted, shepherded by sleek Morag
> Over the heath to school.
> The croft you bought
> For them to share with us
> At Etive's head,
> The crafts and skills we'd learn
> And music play and sing,
> Your pipes a herald through the glen.

Yet feared my heart
The challenge was too great
Did you not promise us the earth?
Was not your courage, when the illness
Cut you down, so God-like
That its power frightened me?
Could I believe
And trusting, face the wind
In equal bravery?
I must not fail.
And when the long ordeal brought you to rest
Taking from me the promise
And the test
Why need I weep?
Your dying left our fragile dream complete.

Numb, and joggling slightly on the stiff and grubby seat of the wartime railway carriage, I headed back after the funeral to my unit. There was a war on, after all, and I had a job to do.

Before I had left Camberly for Norman's funeral, the CO had told me not to bother rushing back. Two of our shows, he reminded me, were recently returned from abroad, but their personnel were away on leave, and Sully could be trusted to look after CWAC discipline at headquarters. Major Purdy had added that since he would be going to London on Friday, he would meet my train, and before he drove me home, we could have dinner together.

"Whatever you choose. Thank you," I had answered. I could not possibly have cared less.

Rai Purdy had been one of the officers for whom I auditioned when the Army Show had played in Vancouver. I had met him next in Toronto, along with other members of the production staff, at a meeting in his quarters, a room at the King Edward Hotel. Because he was in charge of radio–he produced a weekly propaganda broadcast at a CBC studio, featuring the musicians and stars of the Army Show–I saw him only at the evening meetings. Like the rest of the production crew, he was considerably older than I and a professional show-person. Rai had been visibly surprised to learn, as he brought me a rum and Coke and sat beside me on his bed, that I knew nothing about him or his remarkable career. He said he was well-known in radio—indeed, a celebrity in Ontario. Though I felt shy of my ignorance, his bragging had nevertheless astonished me.

I soon gathered that all of the production officers were married, but it took longer to learn why they made a social gathering out of a business meeting and never seemed in a hurry to leave. Rai kept everyone laughing and the other members obviously looked up to him. Perhaps it was he who provided the drinks which followed one upon another without pause as they discussed production problems and arranged rehearsal schedules. Before the company left Toronto to embark for Britain, I knew about most of these officers' marital situations. Rai, for example, had a wife and two children whom he seldom saw; he was anxious to leave Canada because of his unhappiness at home.

In England, it was Rai who made all the production decisions. By that time I was responsible for choreography and show rehearsals. During the first few months, when all five show units were based in the Aldershot area, though Rai was friendly and easy to work with and we were in constant communication, I'd had no personal interest in him. My future was tied to Norman. Losing him left me empty and aimless. Into this abyss walked Rai Purdy.

At around four on that Friday afternoon following Norman's funeral, Major Purdy was standing at the platform gate as my train arrived in London. Seeing him made me pull my shoulders back as I mentally moved into cheery mode. He unslung my haversack and, taking my elbow, guided me to his vehicle. It felt pleasant to be cared for. He decided where we would eat. When he said there was a show he thought we should see the following day, it didn't offend me that he had made reservations—two rooms, of course—at a hotel.

I relaxed and enjoyed a pleasant meal with some ordinary wine. We took our time. Nothing was said about Norman, about the memorial service or his family, and neither Rai nor I remarked on the two of us being in London together. He told me of staff changes and Eddy Sandborne's promotion. He said he had found a stable near Guildford where he could get a horse to ride, asked was I ready to try again, suggested maybe we could ride together.

He talked about the grand feeling it had given him back in Toronto to actually own for a short time a pretty half Arab, obedient and safe, and he described the beauty of early morning in the Don Valley where he had ridden with his dalmatian prior to putting radio station CFRB on the air at seven. I was a good listener, having no energy to enthuse, let alone rise to the occasion with adventures of my own. He talked about the several Russian wolfhounds he had owned. Tovy–Tovarich Odalino II–had been so promising he'd threatened to become a champion. Tovy had been poisoned, and Rai believed it had been the work of some jealous competitor.

He ordered more wine. I drank a little, but weariness had caught up with me. Apologizing, I asked if we might head for the hotel and turn in. He signed us in and took both keys. It surprised me to discover his room was next to mine, but I accepted my haversack and my key from him, said good night and let myself into my room without further conversation. With barely a face-wash I fell into bed and pressed my chin into the pillow to absorb uncontrollable sobs. Perhaps Rai heard them. A while later, when he knocked and I answered the door, he wore the same blue dressing gown I had once borrowed. I needed to be held, and hold me he did while I cried again. And then, as though there was nothing unusual about it, he held the blankets for me to get into bed and lay himself beside me, taking my wretched face in his hands.

I turned away. This was not what I had dreamed and hoped and waited for this long. "I'm sorry. If I have led you to believe I would love you, it was wrong of me. Please leave. Please go now." He did.

Sleep was not willing to comfort me, nor would my eyes stay closed. The events of recent weeks confused themselves with the months and years preceding them. Memories of losses–Pat's desertion, Dad's death and Malcolm's drowning–robbers of life's promises filled the hours of that night. What had I now to look forward to? For whom was I saving my body?

At breakfast I greeted Rai with my usual cheeriness. He asked how I had slept. I avoided the issue. We talked about the weather and discussed finding a park to walk in. The morning passed amicably.

His army vehicle safely parked, Rai found a taxi to take us to the theatre. The seats were uncomfortable. The musical was tired and poor. What were we doing there? I needed to be alone to find my bearings. During intermission we looked down on the smoke-filled theatre-lobby of whatever the forgettable matinee was. Quite unaware of Rai who stood beside me, my mind raced, seeing all those bodies jammed close. It struck me that sooner or later they'd all get their clothes off. Every night, I thought, wrapping my arms around myself, the whole town becomes carnal and I don't belong in it.

Driving back to Camberly, the realization began to trickle through that this attractively alive older man, this actor/producer show person with whom I had worked so closely and well, had been taking care of me through all my difficulties. It was becoming clear, now that Norman was dead, that Rai not only enjoyed working with me, he actually cared for me.

Rai drove in silence as I struggled to hold back a confusion of sadness, shame and fury. When we arrived at the mess, a small fire warmed the sitting room and Cook was preparing a meal. Rai poured us each a drink as he laughingly told the other officers of the appallingly bad performance we had just seen in London. Things were returning to normal.

Christmas passed quietly and in the New Year, as Rai and I tackled increasingly heavy production schedules, my working relationship with him matured. Dance rehearsals kept me occupied for long hours. Often Rai would drop in to see how my work progressed, and his friendly concern for me lessened the ache. We always met at the end of the working day to plan the next day's material. Many times we'd end up in one of the kitchens at midnight looking for a bite to eat.

As I began to know him better, Rai let me in on a bit of gossip that appalled me. He told me that back in Toronto when word had got around about a Vancouver dancer named Sweeny joining the company, the CO had been warned that this girl had a juicy reputation. He must have assumed that I was the Vancouver dancer who, having gone to California to train, ended up as a member of Sally Rand's company of exotic fan-carrying stripteasers. A less self-possessed, less sexy hussy than I had been back then, was unimaginable. We had a good laugh.

Rai and I both suffered from the lack of formal education. Already I knew some of the methods by which he had climbed his theatrical ladder to success without even completing high school. He had told me that until he reached technical school, sitting in a classroom was actually painful for him, saddled as he already was with the name of Horatio. He also suffered from anaemia which made his legs ache and what he called his "hams" itch. Often sent to the corner for fidgeting, he found it impossible to concentrate on the lessons and his grades were always poor.

His father, Lionel, was neither a good businessman nor would he have anything to do with doctors and so Horatio had never visited one. Sometime in his teens, a friend managed to convince him that he was too thin and should seek some advice. Since by this time he'd become a messenger boy and was bringing home enough money from riding his bike to buy the odd sack of coal for the family, he was also able to afford to visit a doctor and get some iron shots which quickly made a remarkable difference.

On the brighter side, I learned that Rai's mother Emily played the piano and had been an amateur actress. Her sister Maud who lived with the Purdys—there were four other children—had graduated from the Royal Academy of Dramatic Art before the family left London to live in Canada. The young Horatio grew up speaking like an actor. The whole family, and as many neighbours as could be regularly recruited, spent their leisure hours during the Depression years writing words and music, rehearsing, building sets and making costumes for the plays they performed in church basements. Rai loved to act and, being a good mimic, learned a whole routine of comic songs which he offered to sing for a few dollars per performance at social affairs and dinners.

He once bragged to me he'd worn out several sets of tails. "Wore spats in those days, too. Carried a spear as an extra with Sir Martin Harvey's company."

Horatio got to know all the budding actors in town and was soon directing plays as well as acting at Hart House Theatre. To get his first radio contract from Harry Sedgewick, owner of CFRB in Toronto, Horatio had to agree to drop his English accent and change his name. As Rai Purdy he had many radio successes and eventually became drama director for CFRB. His best known series was "Out of the Night," a terrifying late-night drama in which he played many of the parts as well as being the show's director and producer. After becoming one of the best-known personalities on the air in Ontario, he launched Rai Purdy Productions Ltd. with further network successes. All this he told me without a speck of humility. Fortunately, I recognized his survival skills as he did mine and we made allowances for one another.

I already knew that most of the officers attached to our company in the thirty-five-to-forty-something age range had wives in Canada, and that some, like Rai, had left behind failed marriages. No doubt they wrote letters full of promises to their waiting women, but in the meantime they had found for themselves temporary replacements—British wives or widows of servicemen—whom they brought to the mess. It made me sad but I guessed it would all straighten out at war's end.

Since Rai and I worked as a team for many hours a day, it was natural that our familiarity continued off-duty. It was assumed—quite automatically it seemed—by the other officers in our mess that I was spoken for by Rai. He had taken care of me when Norman was ill, and in the months that followed Norman's death, our demanding and creative production partnership as well as our friendship were Godsends. Rai even looked to me as he would to a wife for advice on entertaining visiting officers.

I believed I only wanted to be important to somebody, wanted to be seen as attractive. But Rai must have guessed I would capitulate. He left the decision to me. Mere weeks later we spent a weekend in London, and although I came away with some unquestionably negative feelings about our decidedly sealed partnership, I kept them to myself.

Although it seemed perfectly natural to most of those around us who were having affairs, my conscience kept after me: He's a married man. How will you face your family?

Our affair was not subtle, nor was it charged with passion on my part, but it fulfilled a gnawing hunger in me. Sadly, it had begun too soon after Norman's death for any healing to have occurred.

Being the only female officer in our unit I was treated well by all the men, who were quite open to me about their infidelities. No one spoke of home. In exchange for my admiration and unfailing support, Rai granted me privileges far beyond my station: a car and driver whenever I wanted one, passes to London, theatre tickets, a gown made to measure in the wardrobe department.

Shortly after the officers' mess had moved to Camberly, the company ranks were augmented by a handsome Quebec bachelor, Captain Maurice Bourque, who wore the black beret of a tank regiment. Maurice, whose title was purchasing officer, was also Maurice the bargain hunter. He had a special flair for acquiring things, usually for free or a bit of barter. The CO quickly put him in touch with Ask-Uncle-Bob who found in Maurice the perfect recipient for black-market goodies. The longer he stayed with us, the more creative, inventive, unconventional and daring Maurice showed himself to be.

I became aware of Maurice's special skills when our mess food improved radically. Eliminating the government middle man he was bartering a portion of our kitchen swill directly to a local farmer who used it to feed his pigs. In return we received real eggs, chickens and other succulent goodies rarely seen on any menu in these war years. At first it was only the officers' mess that benefitted, but gradually Bourque diverted more and more of our particularly valuable pig swill to the whole company's advantage. No one complained.

Despite constant reminders that we were there because of a war, the Camberly officers' mess was in many ways like home. When everyone was in residence, the sitting room, in which a fire almost always glowed, was hardly large enough to accommodate all the officers. In the intimate dining room no one needed to shout at the table. The light was soft and food was served quietly. We trusted the staff, so in this safe atmosphere we could express ourselves freely. Of course, we used given names.

A group of us were in the mess after dinner one evening enjoying drinks by the fire. I was perched beside Rai on the arm of his favourite chair when Maurice Bourque appeared just inside the sitting-room door and clicked his heels to attention. Using Rai's full title, he asked for permission to borrow a staff car.

Quite abruptly, Rai said no. Bourque stormed out, slamming the door behind him. We all heard him thump up the stairs to his quarters. I wondered what had occurred between the two men. We could hear Maurice pulling out drawers and slamming them closed. Then he returned noisily down the wooden staircase. He kicked open the door.

"Major Purdy!" he commanded from outside. Rai excused himself from our chair and moved toward the door. As he came in line with it, a shot rang out. Twisting and moaning in agony, Rai clutched at his chest, and crumpled face-down to the floor. For an awful moment no one moved. Then I rushed to kneel beside him. Not having a clue what to do, I leaned over to put my hands on his shoulders crying; "No!...oh, no!" When I turned, I saw Maurice with the gun in his hand. The SOB was grinning. Rai rolled over, grabbed and hugged me. "I wanted to see what you'd do," he exclaimed. I could have killed him myself.

Early next morning, I went for a walk over a grassy hilltop near Camberly. The air was unusually heavy with the sound of planes and it occurred to me that this extra concentration of aircraft, gathering into formation high over Surrey like a great grey umbrella, might be what everyone had been waiting for—the most deadly of all Allied raids. As I watched and listened, the sky grew darker and darker and the drone of hundreds and hundreds of engines thrummed into my bones. To think of all those lads up there on a mission, and to contemplate the magnitude of the inevitable destruction this raid must deliver was sickening, and yet there was a thrill to it. When I returned from my walk, the orderly-room radio told me I could be right. Allied planes, closed into one great force from every air station in Britain, had already completed two sorties against a secret target and American Bombers were on course for the third attack. I now believe that what I witnessed was the gathering of the last attack on the beautiful city of Dresden. The first two flights had dropped incendiaries, then came the high explosives which utterly flattened eleven square miles of the heart of the city. Deplorable as is any raid, this infamous attack proved to be the stroke that finally broke the morale of the German High Command.

In March 1955, because CASO had again outgrown its headquarters, we packed up and left Camberly. Other ranks (ORs) cleaned and swept, leaving nothing to chance. Never again would anyone charge barrack damages to CASO! We were told our next stop would be a great location. From the garrison town of Aldershot the road to Guildford in Surrey runs north along a high ridge called the Hog's Back. This picturesque carriageway affords wide views of the rich farm lands lying below. Curving down from this crest, a tree-lined avenue leads to an estate called Down Place where a successful businessman, known as the Margarine King, had built a sandstone mansion in the 1920s. CASO finally came to rest in this blissfully quiet place.

CASO village, which surrounded the Down Place mansion, had parking space for our fleet of quarter-ton and half-ton trucks as well as our troop-carrying vehicles. Several extra 22-kilowatt diesel generators—each unit had one—and a half dozen staff cars were parked across the back of the parade square which had once been the front lawn. Behind the mansion the male ORs were quartered in Nissen huts of sizes that slept twenty or forty or eighty. Rather like enormous corrugated drain pipes with windows on either side and a door on each end, they were constructed of metal arches on concrete slabs and erected in rows, rectangles or end-to-end, depending on whether they were to be used for showers, kitchens, mess halls, rehearsal halls, scene shops or music rooms. Three of them were used in a U shape to surround a motor-transport-repair pit; another three-in-a-row became the wardrobe department where Sergeant Helen Gill reigned over a true costume factory, ultimately operating three eight-hour shifts six days a week.

CASO used one half of the main building for an officers' mess and the other for CWAC dormitories. This beautiful house boasted certain 'mod cons' Canadians could appreciate—plentiful bathrooms and hot-water heating. Alas, the Brits hadn't really conquered their fear of central heating, and the Margarine King had settled cautiously for a gas-fired furnace and water tanks located at least fifty feet away from the living quarters. Once the water became hot it had to find its way some distance underground before arising indoors to enter the radiators, by which time the best one could say was, "The chill is off the place." A costly effort at the best of times, heating of this cumbersome nature needed more fuel than even judicious bartering of pig swill could get us and as a result the hours we had heat were limited.

As the only female officer, it was my good fortune to inherit the master suite at Down Place. Although the bedroom furnishings were altogether basic, I had exclusive use of a huge, well-appointed bathroom en suite. The green fixtures, set in a floor of brown cork tile, were loud but cheery. An immense, totally glass-enclosed tub had spray showers from all four corners. There was also a bidet, but the piece de resistance was a ladder of fat chromium pipes on which to hang wet towels. Providing the heating system was in action, those pipes were filled with hot water.

For the first time since becoming an officer, I was assigned—could it have been Rai's idea, or was it automatic with my promotion to captain?—a bat-woman whose name was Marie. This was absolute luxury. A small, quiet, enigmatic private, Marie came from Quebec. I never learned why she had volunteered to serve in the CWAC and by what route she had come to CASO or what, if any, were her ambitions, and I was too preoccupied with my own life to enquire. I can't imagine a better bat-woman—crudely known as a bat-bag—than Marie. She woke me gently with "good morning, Ma'am" as she opened my shutters at 0600 hours. By the time I had showered, she had made my bed. Laid out in readiness were fresh undies, a crisp shirt, tunic with shined brass and my pressed skirt. Shoes that I could use as a mirror greeted me.

At Down Place that year at the height of production, there were as many as three shows at home base, all at different stages of rehearsal, with a fourth unit on leave. As many as six units toured England and several more were in the field.

I had acquired two dance assistants. One worked with me on new material for the first hour, then took over that unit to practice and polish it. The other supervised practice in a second hall until I arrived to see what they had perfected and to give them new material. In a third hall, girls did a warm-up with their line leader before I arrived. We three instructors were spread pretty thin when production was at its height, but the dancers managed to help each other and worked remarkably well when left on their own. Just as in professional theatre on civvy street, everyone rehearsed until he\she knew the show inside out.

Between one rehearsal hall and another, I would often detour to assess progress in wardrobe, but designer St. John Simpson and wardrobe mistress Helen Gill ran the department so well and were so capable and reliable, I never worried about costumes. Wigs, shoes, hats, make-up, and props were all directly or indirectly Helen's responsibility.

Afternoons were much the same as mornings, though I also had meetings with Sully about CWAC activities, medical appointments, discipline and cleanliness, and meetings with Rai regarding rehearsals in progress. Planning for new productions was scheduled for after dinner and regularly took Rai and me well into the night.

Late one night after rehearsal Rai introduced me to Tiny, who had for some time been chief cook in our big ORs' kitchen. Tiny was immense, and not a well man. We would sometimes come upon him asleep on a chair, centre floor in the hot cookhouse when his evening work was done but the next crew was not in yet. He'd always rouse himself to chat while brewing coffee and making our snacks. Tiny had been in army kitchens seemingly forever. He told us about banquets he had catered as a young man. Although he certainly couldn't have taken up arms as a soldier, he wore a uniform of sorts covered with an enormous apron. Tiny explained that he had faulty circulation, a kind of sleeping sickness. He pulled down his sock to poke a finger into his sickly white calf muscle, then removed it dramatically, demonstrating how slowly the flesh resumed its shape. But Tiny had endurance and spunk. Some time after the unit moved to Down Place, he was promoted to chef in the officers' mess, a less arduous job for him but more fun because he could use his imagination. Every day, with help from Maurice on food supplies, he provided a new and delicious menu. Despite rationing, there were special resources for entertaining in officers' messes and, after Tiny came, we had several quite grand parties. Our most pretentious affair was a seven-course dinner–hand printed menu, candles and all–which was preceded by a cocktail party attended by top brass from CMHQ and elsewhere. Tiny was in his glory.

During that dinner I watched with interest from far down the table how Rai handled the protocol which I knew he had researched with great care. In the place of honour on his left sat my cousin Budge, a Seaforth Highlanders brigadier recently returned from desert campaigns and "tidying up the Italians." He had come down from London to see what I was involved in. On Rai's right sat Colonel Spankey, CASO's representative at CMHQ. Sitting between our adjutant and our purchasing officer–both now wearing the gold crown of a major on their shoulders–were other visiting dignitaries. Ask-Uncle-Bob and war correspondent John Collingwood-Reid sat, as I did, with the junior officers below the salt. As civilian women had not been invited, I was, as usual, the only female in the place.

As there was plenty of liquor, no one felt any pain, which was fortunate as probably no one but I would remember my cousin carrying on about what a wonderful war it had been for him. This led to stories of escapades that turned the air blue and made me blush as my own conscience jabbed me.

When there were civilian women at parties in officers' messes, the ladies usually managed to look quite glamourous. I had acquired a few civvy clothes by then; in addition to those bought in London, I had the long party-dress the wardrobe department had made for me in heavy white crepe, not strapless, but very low-cut, with a huge flared skirt that moved beautifully on a dance floor. Rai liked to show off the few steps he had polished as a teenager under the eye of Cecil de Costa, a Toronto ballroom teacher, and I enjoyed being streaked across the floor, whirled round and round till we suddenly stopped dead!

On special occasions, one mess would invite another to dine or play cards. The sergeants' mess, which included most of the top show people, had a really good spirit for entertaining. They invited all ranks, served wonderful late suppers and, testing new ideas, put on some very funny shows. Rai and I even performed for them a raunchy comedic scene that he had taught me.

One evening the sergeants were in our mess, playing the favourite Army Show pastime, craps, when Rai got on a winning spree. At first it was great fun because he made the wildest bets with impossible odds, blowing on the dice and whispering in a language picked up over many a night out with the boys in civvy street. Risking everything time after time, he kept right on winning.

This seemed to me like a poor show. Several people had begun to look worried. I couldn't leave. The whole thing held a weird kind of fascination for me. I hadn't experienced this kind of addiction, or realized that people could drink so much and still operate so efficiently. It was six in the morning before the tide turned, and seven before Rai rid himself of every last shilling. How the other players fared I can't guess, but it was a relief to me to know that in the end the CO hadn't taken advantage of the NCOs!

Surrey is good horse country, and once CASO was completely settled at Down Place, Rai and I rode on weekends, getting to know a couple of horses at a local stable that CASO later bought and kept for us, temporarily, of course. Rai discovered that as service people we could order correct riding apparel through our QM stores from Moss Brothers in London, which naturally we did. One Sunday morning, Rai shipped our horses to a stable near Albert Hall. We hacked across the High Street and into Kensington Gardens where we were photographed riding with other snobs in Rotten Row. The newspaper caption read: "Colonel Rai Purdy, commanding officer of the Canadian

Army Show, rides with Captain Verity Sweeny, choreographer." The gall of it still makes me cringe.

We also decided the mess needed a couple of dogs and set about finding them. Before long Rai came across a gorgeous English setter at the RSPCA. Simon was fully grown, gun-trained and very friendly. Simon had strayed from his owner to follow the local milkman whose horse had kicked out a couple of his front teeth, barring him forever from the show ring. Unloved and no longer of value, this ex-champion was looking for a new home. From then on, Simon, thrilled to bits to be treated like a spoiled child, followed Rai like a shadow.

I fell in love with an Alsatian pup, four months of age. I called her Flikka after the horse in the movie, *My Friend Flicka*. Obviously I didn't see the title clearly. Each morning, when Marie left my room, she took Flikka on her first outing of the day, returning with a cup of tea for me, memos from Staff Sergeant Sullivan and a request for her own orders. It was unnecessary to badger Marie, who was the perfect bat-woman. I minded my business, and she minded hers.

CHAPTER 11

Endings and Beginnings

On V-E Day, May 8, 1945, Rai and I were on leave in London. Big guns boomed on the Thames and bells clanged in every steeple. Churchill's voice, re-broadcast again and again, confirmed his earlier declaration of peace in Europe. From our hotel room we went out into the street to join the crowd in Trafalgar Square. Thousands of people wandered about, going nowhere special. Some were singing, some embracing. Some lovers, abandoning decorum, had actually wandered from their beds at the news of peace to fuck once more against a rail or on the pavement. Normally I wouldn't have used such a word, but on that day it came to me, and under the circumstances–both international and personal–it felt entirely appropriate. We walked down to Admiralty Arch where bits of ticker tape floated apathetically from grey buildings. I stooped to pick up a piece of this extravagance–I still have it. But there was no wild enthusiasm around us. I saw exhaustion and sadness on many faces. Like them I was grateful that the war was really over, but I was also engulfed by a tawdry, morning-after feeling about my own life.

Back at the mess we did the things expected of officers at such a time of celebration. We waited on the other ranks and, as the booze flowed, people got thrown into the fountain in front of Down Place mansion. NCOs fraternized with privates and the adjutant climbed out of the mess window into a flower bed. But there was an ache to all of the show. The war in Europe had come to an end. Now there was a hell of a lot of cleaning up to do, and mourning and healing. We Canadians no longer belonged here. Something was over that had been a big part or our lives. Soon we'd be going home, separating from the friends who had become important to us.

From moment to moment my own feelings changed from joy to sadness and back to eagerness again. It was a relief to consider the possibility that my life might have a new beginning. I wanted to go home, to start fresh, but when I tried to focus on home there were no clear pictures. I knew that Mum would be waiting in the big old house she had rented in Vancouver, that Moira would be back from the WRCN station in Halifax, and my eldest brother and his British wife and child would come back to Canada, and young Roger would be finishing school. But Malcolm wouldn't be there and neither would Dad. No Norman, my love. Cousin Roderick, Con's brother Dick, and her husband, Rodney, had all been killed. After all my years away, where was home for me?

In the aftermath of V-E Day, weariness, sadness, and anger seemed to sweep over the whole of Britain, affecting everyone. In Aldershot, thousands of Canadian soldiers awaited passage home, but because so many ships had sunk, it could take months before these chaps got a bunk aboard a steamer. With nowhere to go, they had little to do but kick up their heels in Aldershot.

Service people at loose ends can be fearfully destructive. Trouble was inevitable. First, Canuck servicemen smashed one shop window, then another. Then one of the mayor's daughters was given a rough evening. The Canadians began to look like a bad lot. Both British and Canadian officials feared the eruption of a riot. As a result, our job of keeping them entertained was even at least as important as it had been during hostilities. Although some CAS units had already been returned to Canada, others were still touring in England and on the

Continent. These small units, though, hardly made a dent in the need for entertainment to pacify frustrated soldiers piled up in repat depots yearning for home and demobilization.

Rai, however, believed he had a solution, and one night he confided to me his vision of the great show he wanted to produce. It would be "the epitome of troop entertainment," he said. He would call it *Musical Rodeo,* or something like that. His eyes were alight with excitement as ideas came tumbling out. "How about a circus ring for bucking out? We could mix together all kinds of Canadian elements, everything from a lavish stage show to a full-blown rodeo!" He said he would gather in all the small units and create a gigantic show that would take two thousand service people off the streets of Aldershot and maybe even London.

"Where is there a building big enough produce a show like that? Around here, I mean." The concept sounded like fun but I wasn't sold.

"Not a building! A tent! A great jeesly tent!"

"Where would you find that big a tent?

"In Blackpool. They don't use them in winter. Maurice can arrange it." I guessed Rai must have looked into the possibility. Maybe it wasn't so farfetched.

"Will you need dancers?"

"Of course! And horses, as many as we can get." I felt as though my whole body was expanding. "And...and, what about a revolving stage? And bucking chutes and square dancing and curving stairs to a gallery full of musicians?"

I was definitely interested. With increasing eagerness he and I dreamed and schemed for a whole weekend.

Rai could think big. Very big. Since arriving at Down Place as commanding officer, he had risen to his peak of self-confidence. While I had no idea of the difficulties that would be involved in bringing to life a vision so vast as *Rhythm Rodeo*—our final choice of name—I was able to see the reality in his fantasy and could feel and connect with his wild imagination. Fully in charge, he was flying high and, being unable to see why it shouldn't work, I flew with him. We were like kids planning a humdinger of a party. Realizing that this would be the last job we'd do together, I felt it just had to succeed.

In July 1945, Rai had himself and his audacious plan paraded before the Chief of Staff at Canadian Military Headquarters in London. He asked for and received an enormous budget for costumes and sets and enough money to rent a fantastically big tent from Blackpool's famous midway. Maurice was in his element. Rai asked for seamstresses, cooks messengers, drivers and orderly room clerks. He was promised all the extra personnel he wanted to add to his establishment as well as a mass of engineering equipment. Then, due to the increase in his establishment, Rai's rank automatically rose to lieutenant colonel.

The British army sent us a platoon of WACs who had served in Malta, Gibraltar, and other active postings. Grateful to be back in England, these women were not quite ready to be demobilized and they found CAS a piece of cake after what they had been through handling ack-ack guns and the like. They performed the jobs assigned them with gusto, even taking midnight shifts at the sewing machines, driving trucks, typing, cooking, and generally fitting in. Experienced soldiers, these WACs had come from every shire and borough in Britain and spoke with some wild accents! I had to ask for replays on almost everything they said, but we all laughed over it.

On the first day that they paraded with our regulars, Sully and I got the giggles. I couldn't believe the outfits these service women wore—on parade yet! Tams, fore-and-afts, woollen toques, Land Army caps, full battle-dress, summer drill, winter-dress baratheas (with brass and without brass) that were too big or too small. Some wore ties, some jerseys, some had gloves, some were without. They wore skirts, shorts, trousers, socks, stockings, boots, shoes, and men's stuff from all over the show. With the war over, no quartermaster would re-equip them and since they were only lent to us, we wouldn't dare offer them Canadian uniforms. So, take it or leave it, that's how they dressed while they were with us. When inspecting them on parade, it was my duty to question their dress—"Why have you no gloves?" or "Did your quarter-stores run out of official dress?" At this point it was all nonsense anyway, and although I'm sure they answered me politely and correctly, I couldn't understand their responses. Eventually we just smiled at each other.

Most of the remaining hundred or so men and women who made up our overseas units were now ordered back to base. They believed they were homeward bound, but Rai called a parade and stood them easy. He told them he had been given permission to produce the biggest show they would ever see. It would be done under canvas in midwinter, would be a combination music and dance extravaganza plus a fully-fledged rodeo. There would be a thirty-two-piece orchestra and enough power to light a whole town.

The performers were hardly enthusiastic. "He's got to be kidding!" was the general reaction. But when Rai explained that the audience would be two thousand restless soldiers per night trucked in from Aldershot, the old troop spirit kicked in. The show would go on.

Maurice immediately located unworked acreage on a farm property called Pepper Harrow near Godalming, and obtained a grader. Then, under the guidance of a new engineering officer, soldiers began levelling the ground. Soon a huge oval, the shape of a race track, about four hundred feet in length and two hundred feet wide, marked the site where the tent was to go. Within this oval, about one third of the way in from where the back entrance would be, they dug a circular hole and in it onc of our engineers installed a Jeep gearbox destined to turn a revolving stage.

The show needed horses but the Canadian Army Overseas had not shown horses on strength since the First World War. So Maurice, the scrounger, went searching and discovered that there were remount depots—relics from that war—attached to a number of British military establishments around England. From these he begged an assortment of spare animals, anything that might pass as a cowpony or Indian cayuse. There would be chuck wagons, chariots and a stagecoach, and we'd need a few ornery ones as bucking broncos. Without knowing if they would be of any use to us, Maurice also made a deal for a whole family of miniature, pure white circus ponies—and one piebald—plus a team of stocky trick horses. All told, CAS took on seventy-five animals.

I have no idea who found him or whether this slightly obnoxious officer applied because he'd heard what we were up to, but about this time the swashbuckling Lieutenant Colonel Henry "Kit" Carson arrived from a tank regiment, to inspect the stable he was to take charge of. Although this Saskatooner was fresh from a military campaign, he swaggered into Down Place already wearing Western boots and a Stetson. "Le'me git ma leg over some horse-flesh," he drawled. "Ah'll git the buggers moving." (Kit spoke perfectly correct English in the officers' mess.) It seemed as if he couldn't have cared less if he ever got home.

While Maurice's horses arrived by the lorry load, a mountain of saddlery was on its way from the Calgary Stampede. A few young men from Western regiments, volunteers who had forfeited their berths on homeward-bound ships, took over the care and training of the horses as they arrived. Before long they'd built a corral and begun lounging these soft beasts who had spent most of their lives at grass! Some were quite ancient and some would never be fit enough to draw a chariot or pull a stagecoach. By mid-September many more riders and cowpunchers from Western regiments had decided to join us and work the horses at Pepper Harrow.

Rai and I came up with a formula which would feature east-to-west Canadian-flavoured production numbers and alternate between tanbark (the traditional footing for a circus ring) and a huge stage. The development of the show itself depended partly on the talent available—by then, very few performers from the original units were still playing, though some of the senior technicians from early Toronto days had found their way onto headquarters staff and were ready and willing to take on the big responsibilities of lighting and sound and the supervision of putting together the canvases. Among the old timers were: assistant producer, Sergeant Major Hozack, J.; musical director, Company Sergeant Major, (CSM) Bradanovich, T.; costume designer, CSM St. John Simpson, G.; stage manager, Sergeant Leonard, R.; and press relations officer, CSM Cameron, J.W.

The program we dreamed up needed about two hundred performers including thirty dancers on stage plus as many riders. As it turned out, several CWACs were also capable riders. It also needed an extended music department—arrangers and copyists for the thirty-two-piece orchestra, some of whom returned from Captain Farnon's broadcast unit in London—and an additional fifty technicians and stagehands for scene and prop shops and wardrobe. Maurice, by his own magical sleight of hand, supplied fresh costume materials by liberating a whole barge-full of looted European fabrics on its way across the channel to Britain. He never did tell us how he'd done it, but designer St. John Simpson and the wardrobe department were in sequin and lamé heaven.

By September, my two assistants and I were already working piecemeal on choreography in the rehearsal huts, shaping the opening cowgirl production, including the square dances which would take place both on stage and on horseback. Corporal Thompson worked with me on an all-male comedy ballet and I created the numbers called "Carousel" and "Rhapsody." We would have given our eye teeth for a huge hall to put together and rehearse the big numbers, especially the finale with all its horses, ponies and sleighs, but that would have to wait until the stage was built and protected by the tent.

One morning, I arrived at Pepper Harrow to find two huge pylons placed about sixty feet apart somewhat to the rear of the round hole containing the Jeep gear-box. From the tops of both pylons, sections of Bailey bridging sprouted toward each other, growing by the minute. When they met and were bolted together they would form a gallery for the orchestra and provide support for the show's backdrop. Thanks to Maurice's scrounging, this was to be a huge golden lamé curtain.

Standing there on the construction site, I could begin to see it all as it would eventually be. From either end of the gallery, curving staircases would descend onto the stage for grand entrances. All over the canvas ceiling, microphones would hang ready to drop silently wherever the action called for them. Out front, between stage and audience, a grill loaded with spotlights would hang high enough not to interfere with sight-lines. On the left side of the bleachers a glassed-in control room with a good view of the stage and backstage would eliminate the top few rows of seating. Opposite, at ground level, two bona fide bucking-chutes would handle the broncs and bronc-busters. For safety's sake, a strong wire-mesh fence would be put in place immediately in front of the best seats at ground level to protect the audience during the rodeo.

Once the thirty-foot diameter turntable had been installed, the stage–sixty feet deep by eighty feet wide–would grow around it, and behind the stage and the Bailey bridge, Nissen huts for dressing rooms, prop storage, and even a green room would be set up within an oval tanbark track. Two hundred yards behind the tent site, down a gentle slope, I could already see the largest sized Nissen hut being converted into a stable. As I look back and remember the feel of it, I am amazed that we weren't swamped by the undertaking. Sometimes I even had time to enjoy the humour of it.

But it was not all smooth sailing. An incident in late October 1945 reminded me of Canada's ongoing feud between easterners and westerners. At high noon on this day, the temperature stood at two degrees Fahrenheit. At Pepper Harrow, thirty-two miserably cold musicians, refugees from the Toronto Symphony, had been rehearsing on the orchestra gallery high above the stage which was barely protected from the weather by a section of the yet unfinished tent. With good reason to be surly, they were breaking for lunch. Heading for trucks which would transport them to their mess hall, the musicians, bundled in scarves over their military caps and wearing fingerless mitts on their delicate hands, cuddled their instruments trying to keep them warm. As they straggled out over rough ground, a khaki-clad cowboy rode up bareback from the stable leading a dozen riderless horses roped together. They were headed across the large open field to a watering hole at a nearby farm, but to get there, they had to navigate tractor ruts and mud around the site where the tent was still being completed. Seeing the musicians, the cowpoke chuckled and taunted, "Soft suckers!"

With unaccustomed swiftness, a saxophonist dropped his case and lunged at the cowboy. The horses shied and, breaking their tethers, scattering in all directions. With his eye on the culprit, the poke reined in and slithered off his horse. Fists upraised, he approached snarling, "One at a time, you bastards!"

The musicians hurried toward safety.

As October turned into November it became very tense at Pepper Harrow, and about a month before the show was due to open, Rai and I became aware that most of our production staff were depressed. Fearing it couldn't be done, they had lost heart in the show. This knowledge only drew Rai and me closer. We knew we were possibly the only two who still believed in this last pulling together of the Canadian Army Show.

In spite of our sceptical crew, however, two weeks before opening, operations were right on schedule. Costumes were close to ready, horses fit and well in hand. Dug into the ground to silence them, two huge searchlight generators were ready to be hooked up to the lighting board. In the middle of the immense tanbark circus ring—the seating wasn't in yet—the huge stage displayed its central revolving circle of Plexiglass made from aircraft windows. The whole show area had now been enclosed by not one, but two, of Blackpool's largest circular circus tents lashed together to make an oval.

It had rained all day and late that afternoon Rai and I, concerned because a more serious storm was threatening, went to check on the tent and found parts of it still being joined by the 'tent monkeys,' a band of small men over military age who had come down from Blackpool to handle the valuable canvases. Each time the weather changed, the ropes holding together the many overlapping sections had to be adjusted, either loosened when they were wet or tightened when dry, a constant challenge especially in winter. The rain had stopped by this time, but as the afternoon darkened, a wind rose, drying the canvas. Having spent the last several hours loosening wet lines, the monkeys once again scurried up and over the outside of this vast balloon to tighten the lines as the wind dried them. Just inside one of the three entrances to the tent, Rai and I stood surveying this remarkable structure as work lights outside the tent showed us the monkeys' silhouettes through the canvas.

Any ordinary circus tent has one "king" pole, three "queen" poles, and eight to ten outside poles, but the structure surrounding us boasted three king poles, eight queens and more than thirty outside poles. The centre king pole, cut from a giant Norwegian spruce that Maurice had liberated—a term used to indicate rescuing rather than stealing—from the navy, and shortened to fit, rose from the top of the thirty-foot-high Bailey-bridge section that stretched across the back of the open stage. Another king supported the tent halfway back from the stage, and the third was at the outer edge of the bucking ring. The eight queen poles, four on each side of the stage, although usually wooden supports, had been replaced by five-inch steel pipes, each one set into the hollow centre of a concrete block thirty inches in height. A flagged spike at the top of each pole fitted through an opening where it was lashed to the tent.

On this night, however, it was not only flags that were flying. The whole damn tent had begun to fly!

As we stood there it began raining again and we could hear the wind increasing. The monkeys gave up trying to make adjustments and scrambled down. Everything was making its own noise. With each gust of wind the tent lifted the queen poles slightly, then dropped them down into their concrete sockets with a booming sound. It was frightening, but the structure appeared to be safe so far. As Rai and I turned to make our exit, however, an enormous gust struck the tent and we were drawn back to watch and listen as increasing wind sucked the canvas higher and higher, taking the queens with it each time, and we heard the thud and crash, scrape and pound as the poles strained to be released from their concrete bondage. The thirty-odd side poles had been dancing wildly off the ground for some time, but they were light and the tent was strong. It was the queens that could tear the canvas because of their unusual weight.

"God! Look at them!" Rai yelled above the racket. "They're going to jump right out of those blocks!"

"They *are* coming out!" I shouted. "Look! Look at that! There goes another! And another!"

In the eerie glimmer of the outside work lights, an awful and wonderful performance, with its own roaring accompaniment, grander than anything we could have dreamed, took place before us as the tent flew, and the queen poles leapt and thundered and swayed in a magnificent, almost beautiful dance that only we saw. Shaken, Rai and I clung together.

Miraculously, the tent held and held and held until the wind grew tired. When it finally died, the queens stood out in the ring at crazy angles like frozen drunks. Were the poles holding up the tent, or was it the other way around? To our amazement, the tent itself was undamaged. Night had fallen when at last we walked from the tent into the glare of the work-lights, picking our way through the shadows of deep tractor ruts toward Rai's car.

On the Saturday before opening the mounted parade that was to commence *Rhythm Rodeo* tried a dry run—not just around the tanbark where it would eventually take place, but all the way to Aldershot and back—ten or more miles—as a promotion scheme. It was led by cocky Kit Carson on the big black they called Mankiller because he had sent several trainers to hospital. Those horses pulling wagons, chariots and the stagecoach had never navigated anything as steep as the exit road that led up the hill from Pepper Harrow onto the Hog's Back. Once on public roads many of the horses became scared and skittish. However, a few of the cowboys acted as outriders and did a good policing job. By the time we had covered a few miles, the parade seemed orderly, although I have to admit I felt anxious when my horse, behaving as though he'd had enough of this rubbish, tried to bolt. My arms and my seat were tired before we ever entered Aldershot.

As the town had been warned in advance that we were coming, the main street was full of soldiers, all of whom seemed to have remarks to shout at us. We dared not stop to answer questions or socialize in case we got out of order. Luckily, a parade square at the end of the main street was big enough for us to circle around and head in the opposite direction for the journey home. We left Aldershot at a quiet trot. I felt terribly proud of us. We'd all had our hands full keeping it together but now I relaxed, happy to be part of this live advertising.

Then suddenly, not far out of town on a long downward slope, the brakes on the stagecoach failed. Frightened by the coach chasing them, the team took off. Automatically the rest of us took a good hold on our mounts and slowed down as the coach careened away from the middle of the parade, forcing some of us into the ditch as it flew by. From higher up we could all see what was happening. Even though the road flattened out below, the driver was unable to control his horses' speed and struggled just to keep them on the road. In a flash, two outriders streaked by me at full gallop. After something of a chase, these cowboys outrode the coach-and-four and, just like in the movies, one from each side, they jumped onto the lead horses and successfully slowed them down. Our safety angels must have been enjoying it, too, making sure no Morris Minor was heading up the road in our direction.

Neither Rai nor I had given a thought to the possibility of accidents, and despite a near-catastrophe when Kit Carson had his first mounted rehearsal inside the tent with the orchestra and the horses were in a panic. Our luck held. The old saying "hung with horseshoes" fit us perfectly.

Top: In 1945, CASO moved to this mansion, Down Place.

Bottom: A production meeting at Down Place. Left to right: Tony Bradanovich, Rai Purdy, Bill Harding, Helen Gill, myself, and Jim Hozak.

The wardrobe department consisted of Helen Gill, G. St. John Simpson, and a team of talented seamstresses. (NAC, PA 176440)

Wardrobe ran so smoothly that I never had to worry but I did want everything just right. (NAC, PA 150924)

Top: Maurice found us acreage for Rhythm Rodeo at Pepper Harrow, near Godalming.

Bottom: The obnoxious Colonel Henry "Kit" Carson on Mankiller. (NAC, PA 176431)

Captain Riordan and Rita Nadeau on aged remount horses scrounged for the show. (NAC, PA 211715)

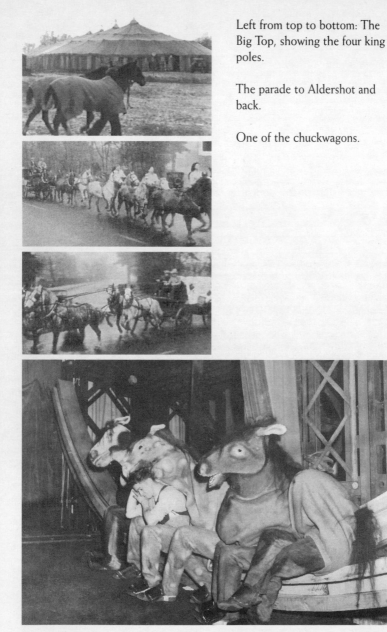

Left from top to bottom: The Big Top, showing the four king poles.

The parade to Aldershot and back.

One of the chuckwagons.

These "horses" were actually a team of crack gymnasts. (NAC, PA 176430)

CHAPTER 12

Rhythm Rodeo: Army Show's Last Hurrah

R *hythm Rodeo* was ready for its opening performance December 21, 1945, at 2000 hours, precisely.

By 1800 hours, troop carriers were already lining up in Aldershot to take two thousand unruly soldiers to see a show in the biggest tent that had ever been raised in England. Since the end of hostilities, local troop entertainment hadn't been up to much. Performers were tired, untidy, unfunny, even gross because the weary show personnel would much rather have gone home. So, on this bleak winter evening, the soldiers would hardly have expected a thrill.

From London and from every Canadian unit in the south of England, officers were also being driven along the rain-slicked roads to this first performance of *Rhythm Rodeo*. It had been the talk around CMHQ for months, since no Canadian entertainment unit had ever had a budget to match it. "It had better be good!" officers had been heard to say.

To outsiders, the *Rhythm Rodeo* adventure might have looked and sounded like a cinch of a job, but it had not been easy. Tonight, however, although even the weather had turned against us, at Down Place spirits were up. Supper was early in all the messes. In a high state of excitement, men and women in the oddest assortment of military and civilian dress, some carrying instruments or props, some of the women in practice clothes with curlers in their hair, hurried in to get something to eat. In the sergeants' mess, three men were breaking up over a new gag they had just added to a comedy sketch. There seemed to be absolutely no military order or discipline but, in show biz tradition, everyone knew *exactly* what he or she had to do. Outside the messes, transport was already waiting to take CASO personnel to the tent. Departure time: 1830 hours.

Fifteen minutes after arrival the girls had already begun putting on their makeup in the dressing rooms behind the stage. Out front, a technician was still up a ladder correcting the position of a spotlight, the only light showing in the gloom of the tent with its vast stage and empty seats. Someone else was quietly testing one of the microphones in the highly sensitive public-address system. A faint burst of back-stage chatter came from behind the enormous, glowing gold curtain that moved gently in the hot air blown through underground ducts from RAF bomber heaters outside the tent. Outside, on either side of the tent, they took the chill off the dressing rooms and stage. It wasn't tropical, but these heaters were considerably better than nothing.

In the stable down the hill, a noisy crowd of horsemen were grooming and dressing an odd assortment of horses. The animals Maurice had gathered had lounged most of their lives unworked and un-cared for, so it had taken much food and hard work in the three months we'd had them to shape them up. One had died from a heart attack while learning to pull a chuck wagonwagon. It had fallen down at full gallop and been dragged forty feet before the rest could be stopped.

Four surprisingly well-matched horses had learned how to pull the stagecoach, a genuine relic of those days though rather too refined for the stubby team that drew it. The 'cow-pony' types, shaped up and shined up, had become accustomed to curb bits and could now even square-dance. It had been Kit Carson's intention to use the smaller, shaggy-coated 'cayuses' as bucking broncos, but the RSPCA forbade the use of synch ropes, prods or burrs, without which incentives even the roughest and most ornery of these beasts had shown no interest in acting like "the toughest broncs ya ever seen." As the result of Kit's boasting, "Thur ain't no horse Ah cain't break," Maurice had made a quick trip to Ireland where he had located some wild, supposedly unbreakable thoroughbreds for Kit Carson and his buckaroos.

For the two girls who rode Roman style with one foot on the back of each horse, the four experienced circus mounts that Maurice had found were perfect. Two comparatively cobbish crossbreeds worked well harnessed for chariot racing. Six of the miniatures, trimmed to the last hoof, seemed to enjoy pulling sleighs much larger than themselves and being led about by the smallest of soldiers dressed as footmen in velvet and satin. Some of that little herd of circus ponies were such miniatures, a man could carry a couple at one time.

While Rai and I had our own horses, Maurice had found a few well-behaved, respectable mounts for those who rode English style. For himself, Kit had successfully tamed Mankiller a wild black thoroughbred. But for all his boasting, the black Irish horse had not given in easily. For Captain E. H. Reardon, his second-in-command, he'd picked a quieter bay. Although none of these horses had ever before worn Western tack, they had all been quickly trained to carry elaborate gear sent from the Calgary Stampede.

In the middle of the stable, the paleskins who would act as native Indians shivered as they sloshed each other with body paint. Waiting around—some loose, some tied—were the shaggy dogs that would follow the travois. Despite the weather, by the time the audience was seated, the parade of all these performers, human and animal, plus the coach and chariots and various wagons would be ready to move up the hill from the stable toward the back entrance to tent.

At 1930 hours, as the lights of the first troop lorry signalled the audience's arrival through the rain, the house lights came on inside the tent. Soon khaki-clad men and women began to ooze through the tent entrances and clamber noisily up and up to the highest seats, hurrying to gain the best vantage points. Several spots splashed light on the massive curtain, backdrop to the stage. Set within the stage, the

turntable was brightly lit from underneath. The two very visible bucking chutes took up a bit of the lower level seating closest to the stage
on the right hand side, but visibility was fine immediately above them.
As more and more soldiers kept pouring in, voices grew louder, were
more openly enthusiastic. At the same time their closely packed bodies began to add warmth and, owing to the wetness of outer clothing,
considerable humidity.

At 1950 hours, backstage just inside the rear entrance to the tent,
we, the officers–except for the CO, who had gone out front to meet
the "red tabs" from London–stood ready to mount our horses. Out
front, after the other ranks had arranged themselves in the bleachers
which took up two thirds of the oddly shaped tent, the officers–from
the chief of staff down–were shown to their seats at ground level.

Control-room lights glowed softly. In the darkness behind the
bridge the musicians, followed by conductor Sergeant Major Tony
Bradanovich, made their way up steep stairs to take their places on the
orchestra gallery above the stage. Hurrying backstage to where his
horse was held, Rai mounted. By this time, the body of the parade
which he was about to lead was well on its way toward the tent from
the stable.

The house lights dimmed a little, then a little more. Behind the gold
curtain, the twenty-four dancers ready to perform in the opening number, having checked each other's make-up and costumes, moved
silently into position.

As the house lights went to black, show lights hit the gallery and a
spot irised in on the conductor. Turning to confront the musicians, he
lifted his baton. As the first notes of "O Canada" brought everyone to
attention, a thrill sent shivers down my back. I felt enormous pride in
being Canadian. The audience had hardly sat down when fanfare trum-
pets shouted: "Hang on to your hats! Here we go!" and rolling drums
signalled the beginning of the grand parade.

To the wonderful circus music, "Gaily Through the World,'
Lieutenant-Colonel Rai Purdy, Canadian Army Show's Commanding
Officer, at a sitting trot on his dazzling chestnut, led the parade with

pomp and ceremony. He was closely followed by Lieutenant-Colonel Kit Carson, officer in charge of the rodeo, riding Western on his magnificent black hunter beside his rodeo second-in-command, Captain Reardon. I rode behind with several other officers, feeling the bulk of the parade closing the gap behind us as they poured in through the back entrance. By this time the head of the parade had advanced around the ring and was proceeding across in front of the stage. A barrage of light came up on the scene as the gait of the horses began to increase. The audience could now see past the officers in the lead to a pair of Roman chariots driven by rugged, spread-legged, charioteers. Leaning back, they held their reins with their left hands and carried long whips with the right. Following them came a loping posse of cowboys, then a couple of noisy chuck wagons, with their horses champing for a race and their wheels throwing up mud as they rounded the curve.

The parade was gathering speed as two girls, tandem Roman riders—flexing their knees to keep in stride with their four eager mounts—rode barely ahead of the magnificent stagecoach with outriders. There followed several bandits and sheriffs, plus a crowd of almost naked 'Indians' riding bareback. The last Indian pony dragged a bumping travois on which sat a large blanketed matriarch played by one of the men. Tied-on cooking utensils clunked and dragged next to a lean, shaggy dog on a leash, with two other dogs running loose beside it. By the time the travois actually came into view, the beginning of the parade had travelled around behind the stage, and the CO on his chestnut cantered nose to tail with the travois, completing the circle.

By this time the parade was really moving!

Unfortunately, the seam where the two tents joined ran right across the canvas ceiling about halfway between the stage and the fence protecting the senior officers. Despite the efforts of the monkeys, this seam wasn't very waterproof. As it had been raining hard, the tanbark had become dark and thoroughly soggy, and the wire fence did nothing to shield those officers seated at ground level from what was coming their way. Their red tabs had been clearly visible at first, but as the speed of the parade continued to increase–the orchestration punctuated with cymbal crashes and trumpet flourishes–horses and wagons and chariots and the stagecoach all hugged the curves, and more and more soggy wet tanbark flew straight at the officers in the first few rows. The crowd roared its approval, but I knew Rai must be dying. By the time the whole parade had completed another circle, the red tabs of the senior officers were completely camouflaged with mud. The other ranks howled with delight, and so, thank God, did the senior officers. The whole place was aroar! Later, after some serious questioning, we decided to leave the senior officers' seating right where it was!

After the third time round, the parade exited where it had come in at the back of the tent, only this time at full gallop. Once outside, the commanding officer circled his horse sharply away from the others, ready to re-enter. The lights were going down, and as soon the travois was safely out, Rai came barrelling in and slid to a stop centre front where a spotlight focused on him. His horse, catching sight of the microphone descending on its motorized cable, backed away and began dancing just as Colonel Purdy, nonchalantly waving at the servicemen, shouted:

"Anyone here want to go home?"

It took them a second, then, wham! They all shouted at once: "Y-E-E-E-E-S!!"

It was sheer luck the CO didn't hit the tanbark. His excited horse reared straight up, pawing the air like Silver. The crowd roared their approval and, by another stroke of luck, he got the hell out of there in one piece. "Should'a wore spurs," taunted Colonel Kit, as Colonel Rai flew past him out the rear exit.

Our show was off to a great start. The twenty-four cowgirls in their cute short costumes designed by St. John Simpson–pale blue leather skirts with white fringe trim, white gauntlets, boots and Stetsons–poured onto the stage through a central divide in the gold curtain. Each one started to spin a snowy white lariat as she ran into place to sing and tap dance to "Don't Fence Me In." Then a bunch of cowpokes moseyed in on the tanbark on either side of the stage. Dismounting, they tethered their horses to queen poles and climbed up to join the girls on stage where they all danced and sang the familiar words together. The production number then became a square dance—the inspiration of Private Len Houle from Courtenay, B.C. a Western rider, roper and square dancer—and moved back to the tanbark when the fellows left the girls on stage and remounted their horses to "show 'em how it's really done." The mounted riders did an allemande left and spun their partners, the riders linking arms, while the horses, nose to tail, pivoted on the forehand. The horses bowed! Then cantered off. Much noisy applause from the bleachers as the cowgirls ran up the grand staircases and disappeared from view.

Now, a bunch of soldiers in battle-dress, caps, webbing and big black army-issue boots came running through the curtain onto the stage, fell in to a super-straight line, made a noisy right dress and eyes front before unfolding mini-ostrich fans from each hand and performing a parody of a nude dance. I had swiped this number from one of the smaller units where it had been done with gusto by only four men. They performed a kind of semaphore, covering—with any luck—each other's 'privates.' This group did it really well with all the facial expressions of coyness and embarrassment that made it a hoot. The orchestration helped by emphasizing each obvious error in the placement of fans.

Next to appear on the tanbark were the Roman riders, standing one foot on each of their two horses. The girls kept the horses at a steady canter, cleverly coaxing them to move in time with the music. On the second time around they circled right and left reversing positions, doing serpentines in opposite directions until they were once more lost to sight behind the stage. When next they appeared, the horses were four abreast and when they reached centre the girls swung them around to halt facing the audience. Before leaving, the two pairs cantered opposite figures of eight crossing at the centre of the tanbark twice and then left the tent at a controlled gallop. I knew enough about dressage by then to create this little dance for the riders.

With the stage in darkness while the girls rode, the stagehands set a solid white curb around the circle of Plexiglass. The first lights to come up were from beneath the glass, cool and blue and flickering with white from bulbs equipped with spinners. The revolving stage had become a swimming pool complete with white handrails and ladders for entering the water. On the two grand curving staircases posed dancers in flowing cloaks of emerald velvet.

I had choreographed this one, billed in the program as "Rhapsody in Blue, Yellow and Green," with music by Gershwin, to suggest synchronized swimming. As the girls came down the stairs, lights caught the glint of bare legs and shiny yellow-and-blue swimsuits. When the cloaks came off, the dancers slid onto the liquid-looking pool on their stomachs to form geometric patterns as if they were swimming and the turntable began to slowly spin. Rolling and somersaulting, the girls closed in to centre and then opened like a flower. As the turntable gained speed, the whole flower became a blur, and when it came to rest the girls popped up around the outer edge to sit upon the curb. Looking wet in their plastic swimsuits, they waved to the audience. After applause, the dancers retrieved their cloaks and, wrapping themselves coyly, mounted the stairs as the lights faded.

A spotlight next picked up a lone, black-clad horseman entering at a gallop. This outlaw was barely out of sight behind the stage when outriders from a stagecoach came streaking after him. But they'd missed their man and they too, had disappeared from view as the jostling carriage with its squeaky wheels and clanking harness came into sight. As the horses hurried the carriage forward, the coachman cracked his whip and yelled at his horses, but moments later the bandit overtook it, jumping onto the lead horse. By the time the outriders had galloped around behind the stage to arrive at the scene, the coachman was already begging for mercy. A gentlewoman passenger in a crinoline, having thrown open the carriage door, was about to jump from the top step when shots were fired, the bandit fell, and one of the outriders rescued the lady, sweeping her onto the saddle behind him as he flew by. Exit everyone at the gallop.

When lights next came up on the turntable at centre stage for "Summer Carnival," an honest-to-goodness steam calliope puffed and blew, making thumpy, watery music from the heart of a painted carousel. The calliope had been liberated by Maurice from another barge of loot on its way from Europe for sale in England. The addition of lights flashing on gilt and mirrors, circus barkers and crowd noises created a cheerful atmosphere. Six realistic horses moved slowly up and down as the carousel revolved. On the back of each horse rode a pretty girl. Round and round they went until the scene was set then, as the turntable slowed, the horses suddenly reared up, shedding their riders who ran off screaming.

The horses then shambled downstage to make a front-legged bow to the audience. Inside each horse were two men, part of a slick team of Canadian air force athletes whom Maurice had contacted in repat. The strength and ability of the men in this team had made choreography for "Summer Carnival" my easiest task. I came on in the snappy costume of a ring master, cracking a long whip and directing these clowns into a crazy kick routine, front legs, then back legs. They reared and bucked, did turns on the forehand, cantered in pairs and simulated the charge of the Royal Canadian Mounted Police Musical Ride. When they had shown off enough, I let them have fun playing at the edges of the turntable which had begun to rotate again. With their left feet on the turntable, they paddled with their right feet as though on scooters. At the crack of my whip they jumped and, changing legs, paddled backwards. Then, both front legs on, back legs off, running to keep up, and vice versa, the front legs performing shoulder in, crossing and uncrossing to keep up with their own rear ends! To finish, they all reared, the back halves lifting the front, and staggered downstage as though a horse could walk on two legs, plopped into a bow, then turned and bucked before galloping off. Later in the show these same guys—without the horse costumes—had a slick gymnastic spot of their own.

One of the gentler productions in the show was a rather old-fashioned presentation of a Dutch village called "Holland Memory." Windmills and all those romantic things, which in no way represented the Holland our soldiers had witnessed, made light of the sad reality. All the dancers wore clogs. The boys, in blue baggy pantaloons, wore full white shirts and black bargeman's caps, and the girls in white stockings and those lovely full print skirts carried flowers in their white aprons. From stiff winged caps, yellow braids swung and bobbed. This look back at picture-perfect Holland brought tears to many eyes.

When "Holland Memory" came to an end on stage, lights dimmed and music faded. From the darkness a cowboy yelled, "Git in thar, ya li'l bugger." Then a beam of light revealed a poke sitting on top of the first bucking chute waving his hat. Slapping the boards of the high fence, he kicked his heels noisily inside the chute and shouted at the ornery critter to wake up and show some spirit. Another poke appeared atop the fence on the opposite side, also hat in hand, ready to descend onto the bronco for the first demonstration of bucking out.

While these preparations went on, Kit Carson loped in and the two pick-up riders who followed him shut gates on either side of the stage to enclose the bucking area. Kit's mike came down and he announced grandly, "This horse ain't never been rode before." More noisy shouts, more banging on the boards. A third cowboy climbed up over the chute gate about to swing it open when the first cowboy called to the audience:

"Watch out! They're comin' out!"

The first competitive rider dropped out of sight and we knew we were in for excitement. Lots of slapping. Lots of shouting. The gate swung wide and out came a cowboy on his hands and knees with the smallest piebald pony imaginable straddling his back.

Roars of laughter. The cowboy galloped to the centre of the tanbark and slipped out from under his horse. Carefully picking it up in his arms, he got out of the path of the next competitor who was to come out of chute number two. This promised to be the real thing. More noise, much banging and shouting. This time it was a snappy little cowgirl who descended into the chute, also hat in hand.

The second gate was swung wide and a wild animal careened out, bucking, rearing, twisting, and jumping but it turned out to be another laugh. Two of the gymnasts back again in a horse costume gave the cowgirl a real ride. As a pick-up rider moved in to save her, the comedy horse kicked out blindly at the real pick-up horse, accidentally making contact. With extraordinary calm, the pick-up horse looked around to see what had hit him just as a photographer from *Pathe Gazette* caught this ridiculous moment on film to show around the country in the cinemas.

The audience hadn't stopped laughing when the banging began again. Chute number one was set to open, this time for real. The nonsense out of the way, Colonel Kit Carson introduced the rider in the chute in his best cowpoke drawl, "This here rider you're gonna see nixt, ridin' Skyrocket imported from Ireland, is Gunner Trottier from my home town, Maple Creek."

The big red horse came out spinning. Not a small rough pony but a huge Irish hunter out to kill! No cinch ropes, no prod or burrs, just the lad on top with his hat in his hand and his spurs flying, up on the neck, then behind the girth! Once, twice, three times, four times! The crowd went wild. Still hanging on, the cowboy was retrieved and the horse controlled. We were more than ready for the next.

This time it was one of the remount horses that had shown spirit and been goaded to behave badly. He certainly came out in a hurry, but dug his hocks under him and slithered to a stop, staring around with "What the hell's all this?" written all over him. The cowboy tried to kick him alive but the poor frightened thing had no spunk left.

Next out was a horse that really danced, quickly dislodging the rider. Too bad! It looked like fun but the next gate was about to open. This ordinary bay was another of the big Irish hunters, and the boy who rode had a reputation from way back. Kit called him "Moses (Midnight) Ned from the Caribou." What a performance! What an exciting ride! He got dumped, but not before "puttin' on a real good show," and without using a bucking cinch. Wow! Just what the crowd was looking for!

To give the pick-up riders a rest, a cowboy on the stage dazzled everyone by spinning lariats of several sizes, then after the pokes had bucked out several more rodeo broncs, the ring gates swung open for a chuck wagon race. Kit told us that one driver came from a Calgary regiment and the other from Sault Ste. Marie. The audience naturally took sides, so there was a lot of shouting. The race was won by Trooper R. W. Armstrong from Sault Ste. Marie.

When the bucking was over, the tanbark empty and the ring lights had gone out, a snow scene like an old-fashioned Christmas card appeared on stage. Music with sleigh bells and chimes accompanied this static scene of snow-covered trees and skaters on a frozen pond with a tiered fountain at its centre. The picture included a snow man and piles of snowballs and six elegant silver sleighs, each drawn by a snow-white Shetland pony in silver harness. Six footmen in powdered wigs, clad in ice-blue velvet tunics and white satin britches held the six ponies. One glamorous showgirl sat on the high seat in each sleigh, adorned in lamé with feathers, satin with rhinestones, or velvet with white fox fur. Each was motionless except for the sparkle of her sequins or jewellery. Though happy Christmas music filled the air, nothing moved but a pony's tail.

The picture deserved applause and got it. Then it came alive as the orchestra introduced the finale. This was a new holiday song written by Tony Bradanovich with lyrics by the CO. The words accompanied the action on-stage. The ponies, led by the footmen, drew the six sleighs clockwise around the pond while a complete ice ballet took place on the now blue turntable spinning anti-clockwise to give speed to the dancers' skating. At the conclusion of the ballet and the sleigh song, dancers brightly dressed as children, came running down the staircases with their hands full of snowballs which they pitched all over the stage.

One by one, the sleighs with the show girls arrived at the front of the stage, where each mannequin descended from her sleigh to do a little fashion parade before taking her place on the fountain at centre ice. The grooms kept the ponies circling the pond until all the show-girls, the skaters, and the kids were in the final tableau; then they took steady positions facing the ponies inward toward the centre, each in a separate spotlight. The turntable once again rotated slowly, and the bright lights dimmed so that a mirror-ball could flash rainbow colours on this last wintry scene.

Seasonal music continued and spotlights came up upon the entrances as, from both sides of the stage, all the riders flooded onto the tanbark. The show came to its end when the horses and everyone onstage formed up and stood at attention, as did the audience, for "The King," and once again, "O Canada." Everybody sang.

Without observing the protocol of silence after the anthem, our standing audience let us know they'd had a good time—so much so, many of the horses got skittish. Even Kit's horse misbehaved. Backing around in a circle it reared straight up. Looking as though it would go over backwards at any moment, it emptied Kit quite slowly out of his stock saddle onto the tanbark! I knew a few people who must have wanted to shout, "Hooray!"

Rhythm Rodeo played to a full house on twenty-two occasions within the next four weeks, which means that our audience totalled more than forty thousand. After opening night, the most rewarding performance was the Christmas show to which we invited all the local children and their parents. The way their eyes shone made us proud and happy.

EPILOGUE

The joy of homecoming in the spring of 1946 was somewhat tempered by sadness as, one by one, we Sweenys returned to Vancouver. Mum had rented a grand old Kerrisdale house where she and my youngest brother Roger, now ready for Royal Roads Naval College, welcomed Moira from the WRCNs, Sedley from the Royal Engineers, and me from the Army Show, as well as Sedley's wife Diana and their daughter Nicola. It was great to be together again but we were reminded, especially Mum and I, that Dad was gone and Malcolm was still missing. I had lost my best beloved. When I tried to find old friends, they just weren't there and my life seemed to have no direction. With Moira's help, however, dance once again came into focus.

In 1947 my ex-commanding officer, Rai Purdy, became my husband. From then on, thanks to Rai's particular skills, our work together, and considerable fancy dancing, doors opened for us into a world of travel and adventure. Despite their lack of roots, our children Heather and Roger thrived, and the stories we share cover the forty-three years Rai was with us. I have tried to squeeze them all into my next book, called *Fancy Dancing*. Book One, published in 1998 by Heritage House, is called *The Luckiest Girl In The World*.

As entertainers and soldiers, the men and women who travelled to theatres of war with the Canadian Army Show performed an invaluable service to thousands of troops during the Second World War.

This book reveals the laughter, heartache, and fortitude behind the scenes of the Army Show. It is the story of Verity Sweeny—dancer, choreographer, soldier, and finally, at war's end, a survivor. Between 1943 and 1946, she made considerable contributions to the Army Show and worked side-by-side with such colourful personalities as Shuster and Wayne, Roger Doucet, and Jimmy Shields.

Other titles available in the Voices of War Series:
A Soldier's Diary
Bomber Pilot: A Canadian Youth's War
Line Shoot: Diary of a Fighter Pilot

ISBN 1-55125-051-9

9 781551 250519

IN CANADA
$19.95

Vanwell